Art's Biggest Stage

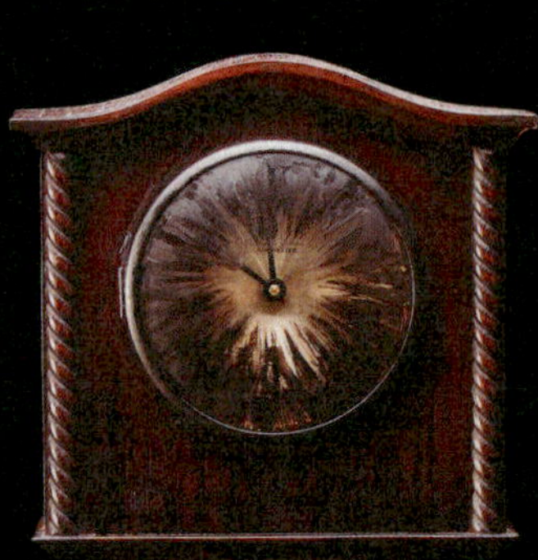
END
-ings
ARE
THE
NEW
BEG

Art's Biggest Stage

Collecting the Venice Biennale, 2007–2019

Brian Sholis

with contributions by
Sarah Hamerman and
Susan Roeper

Clark Art Institute
Williamstown,
Massachusetts

Distributed by
Yale University Press,
New Haven and London

Contents

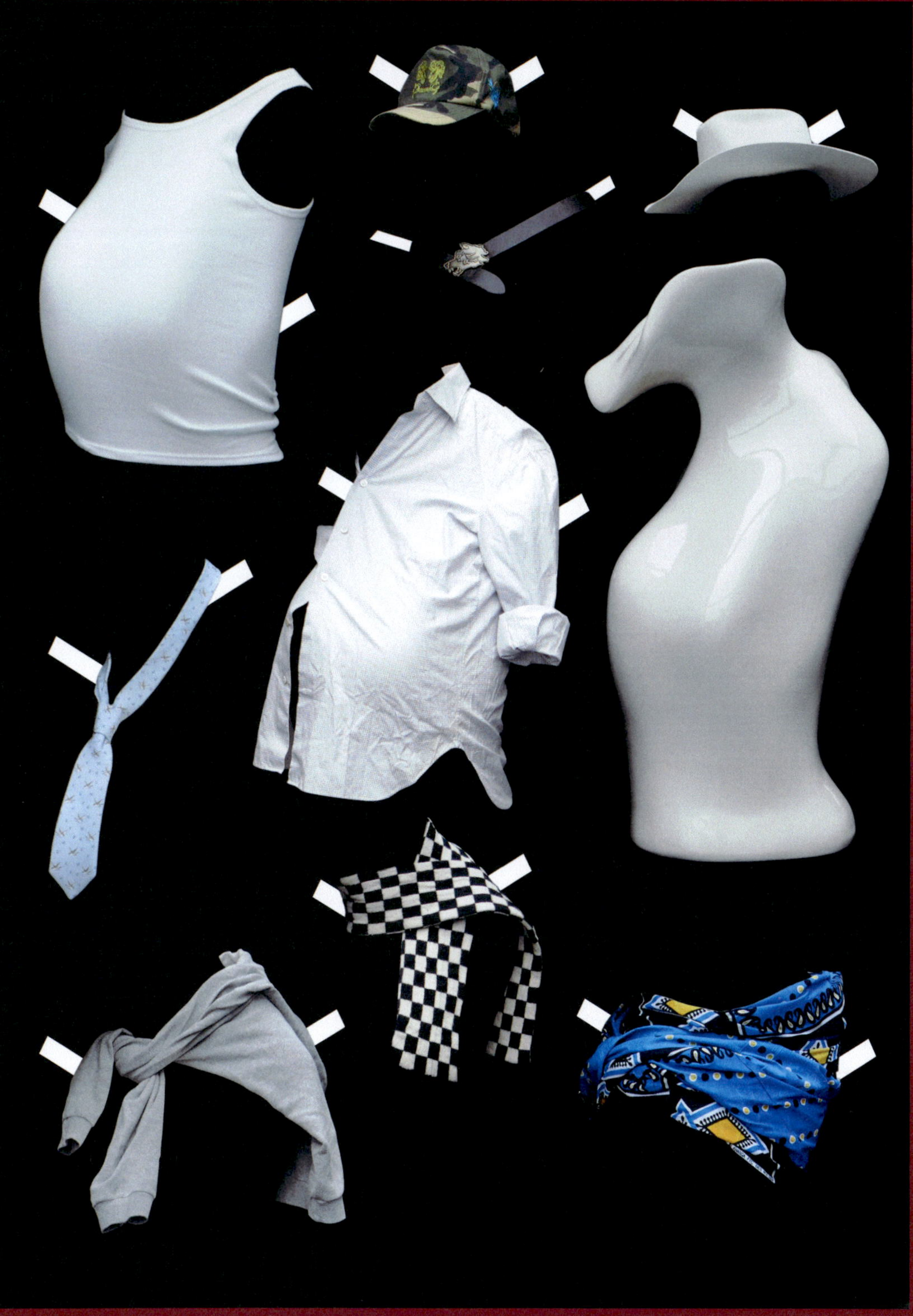

Director's Foreword

As the world becomes increasingly globalized, international art exhibitions and biennales have attained unprecedented importance. These showcases invite visitors from around the world to engage with some of the most significant art being produced today. The most prestigious of these events is the Venice Biennale, wherein designated national pavilions exhibit works by leading contemporary artists, while a host of other elaborate artistic displays materialize in venues throughout the city. Attending this event is a particular privilege given its impermanence; at the end of each Biennale, the crowds disperse and the art is packed away. Nevertheless, to be present at the Venice Biennale, whether as a member of the public or an insider of the art world, is to gain insight into the most crucial movements and dialogues taking place in the arts.

Art's Biggest Stage: Collecting the Venice Biennale, 2007–2019 is an effort to capture the physical, yet ephemeral, manifestations of those movements and dialogues. For the past twelve years, the library of the Clark Art Institute has been collecting traces of the Biennale: posters, tote bags, books, and more that accompany, publicize, and commemorate the extravagant Venetian displays every other year. These remnants, generally neglected once the event is over, tell a story about the Biennale; they are, in effect, vital records of the contemporary art world.

These objects are natural, if perhaps surprising, additions to the Clark's library, which has long been a heralded site for art historical research. The Venice Biennale collection complements the array of existing resources by offering additional insights into the field of contemporary art. It is my hope that this collection, and the exhibition that draws on it, will encourage bold ventures into exciting new areas of research.

This project is twelve years in the making, and I thank the tireless and adventurous Thomas Heneage, the Clark's partner in obtaining these materials, for his resourcefulness in gathering the objects in the Venice Biennale archive. I also applaud the Clark library staff, Susan Roeper and Terri Boccia in particular, whose bold, forward-thinking initiative and foresight led to the creation and preservation of this wonderful collection. I am grateful for Brian Sholis, who thoughtfully curated *Art's Biggest Stage*, as well as the exhibition's designers Jarrod Beck and Heidi Humphrey. Credit is also due to the authors of the essays in this volume, who include Brian, Susan, and Sarah Hamerman. Finally, I thank Denise Littlefield Sobel, Maureen Fennessy Bousa and Edward P. Bousa, and Amy and Charlie Sharf for providing the financial support to stage one of the Clark's most complex and daring exhibitions.

OLIVIER MESLAY   Hardymon Director of the Clark Art Institute

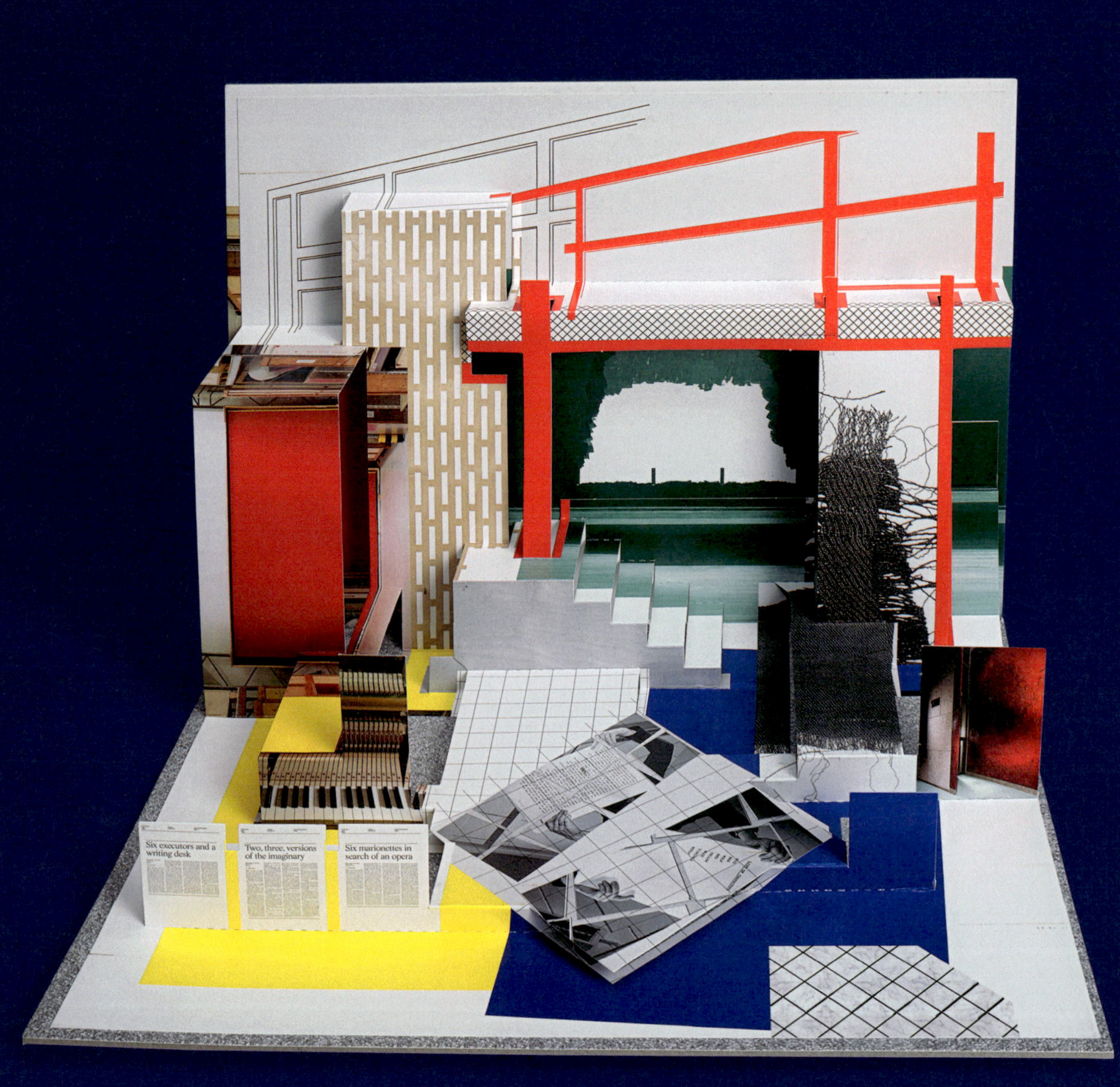
Six executors and a
writing desk
Two, three, versions
of the imaginary
Six marionettes in
search of an opera

Collecting the Biennale

SUSAN ROEPER

The Clark's library has a collection of publications relating to the Venice Biennale that dates back to the event's beginning in 1895. Historically, the primary publication has been a catalogue that accompanies the international exhibition—once a juried show, but now with an appointed artistic director. With the introduction of national pavilions in the early twentieth century, each with its own exhibition and collateral events approved by the artistic director, the number of publications expanded greatly. Some of these catalogues have been relatively easy to acquire as the publishers have had strong means of distribution, but others are published in limited print runs by small, independent publishers who did not have the goal or resources to distribute them internationally. This has been especially true with artists' books—a genre in which the Clark's library has a particularly keen interest. Often, these publications are available only in Venice during the course of the exhibition, making them difficult for many libraries, including the Clark's, to obtain.

For the Clark's library, that all changed in 2007, when London book dealer Thomas Heneage, the Clark's acquisition's librarian, Terri Boccia, and I, hatched a plan. Thomas would be attending the opening

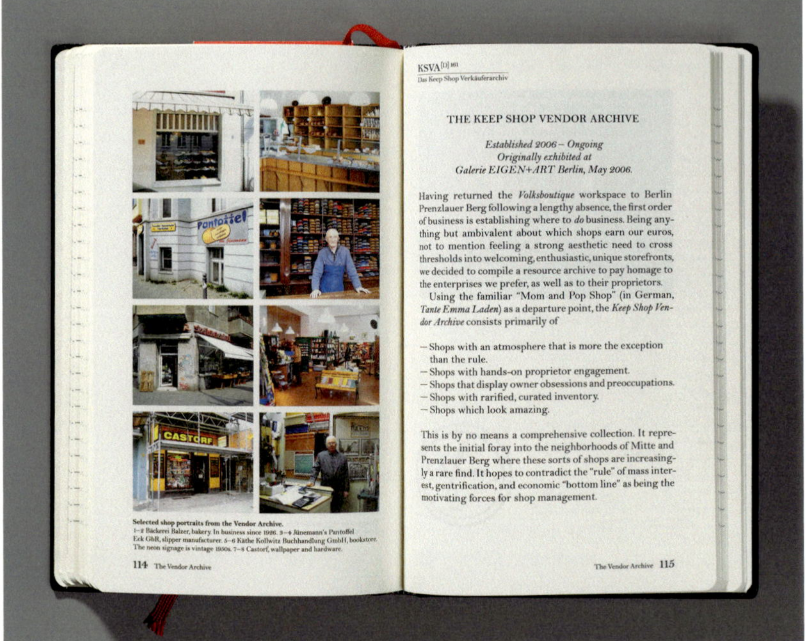

FIG 1 | CAT 44 Christine Hill (American; b. Binghamton, 1968), spread from *Minutes*, artist's book from the main exhibition of the 52nd Venice Biennale, 2007. 8 ⅜ × 5 ⅜ in. (21.3 × 13.7 cm). Clark Art Institute Library, Artists' Books Collection

events, or *vernissage,* with his wife Carol Vogel, then an arts editor for the *New York Times*. Typically, those fortunate enough to obtain a coveted press pass will receive invitations to parties and events attended by artists, dealers, collectors, and other VIPs. It is at these events that many publications are first available, if not distributed outright as gifts. Heneage would use his access and wiles to obtain what he could for the Clark's library. This first foray resulted in nearly two hundred publications, including Christine Hill's artist's book *Minutes* (fig. 1)*,* as well as invitations, announcements, and press kits—brochures containing artists' biographies and images for reproduction. We were thrilled with the publications and certain that our plan had been a success. But did we want to keep the ephemera? The library's collection-development policy did not include such materials. We took a wait-and-see attitude, and in the planning for 2009, we encouraged Heneage to snag for us whatever material he could.

The bounty gathered that year secured a definite place for ephemera in what would become the library's Venice Biennale Ephemera Collection. My email inbox from June and July was flooded with subject lines like "Salami" and "Meat product/Art work." The former were initiated by Heneage, who upended the tote bag he had brought back

　　　　　　　　　　　　　SUSAN ROEPER

to his hotel in Venice from a visit to the Nordic and Danish pavilions to discover—among the variety of press materials—a salami. The pavilions that year, created by the artists Michael Elmgreen and Ingar Dragset and titled *The Collectors*, situated the venue as an open house at the home of an art collector, with visitors playing the role of potential homebuyers. The tote bag, distributed to the first five hundred visitors, contained multiples, or editioned works of art or books, commissioned by the artists whose work adorned the walls of the collector's home (fig. 2). One of these multiples was the aforementioned salami, the contribution of conceptual artist Maurizio Cattelan. Heneage emailed me asking if we wanted the salami, or if he should just eat it. I replied that we wanted it—or at least I thought we did. Thus we began working with the Clark's registrar, Mattie Kelley, who agreed to try and arrange a legal way to bring it here. We gave up on such efforts when we could not satisfy the United States Department of Agriculture's requirements, but we have the denial letters (fig. 3), which in some ways are so much more appropriate than having to care for the actual salami. Randy Kennedy of the *New York Times* was so amused by this story that he wrote about it for his newspaper's coverage of the Biennale later that summer.[1]

In 2009, Thomas also began to send us ephemeral digital content. The press kits from the Netherlands and New Zealand arrived not as

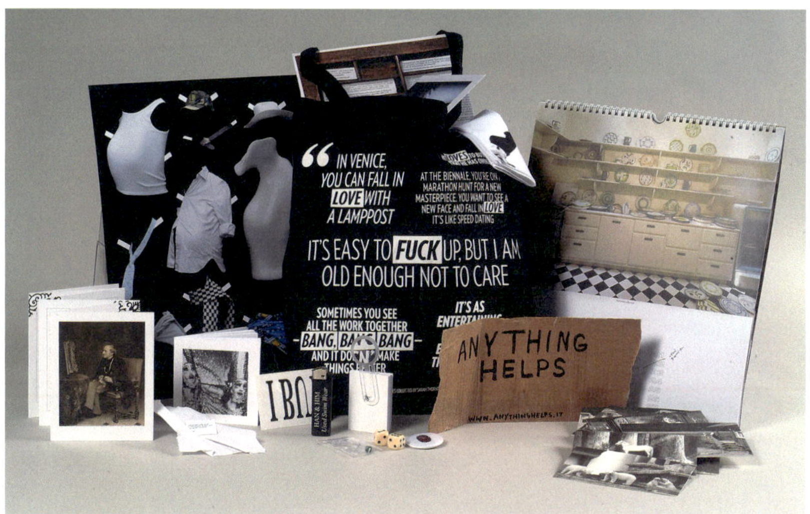

FIG 2 Michael Elmgreen (Danish; b. Copenhagen, 1961) and Ingar Dragset (Norwegian; b. Trondheim, 1969), an assortment of objects from *The Collectors*, Nordic Pavilion of the 53rd Venice Biennale, 2009. Clark Art Institute Library, Venice Biennale Ephemera Collection

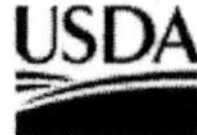

USDA

**United States
Department of
Agriculture**

Animal and Plant
Health Inspection
Service

Veterinary Services

National Center for
Import and Export

Animal Products

4700 River Road
Unit 40
Riverdale, MD 20737

Telephone:

FAX:

Sterling and Francine Clark Art Institute
225 South Street
Williamstown, MA 01267

Monday, August 10, 2009

Our office has completed an initial review of your request for the importation of Meat - the import would contain 1 Salami, 225 grams, that is part of an original artwork by renowned Italian artists exported from Italy. Your request was assigned reference number ▨▨▨▨▨.

Based on the information submitted by your establishment, our office has determined that we can not process your request at this time. Our office is requesting the following information:

1) Provide us with a health certifcate from the **animal health official of the National Government** of Italy with **details of the origin of exported product**.

Fax the requested information to my attention at ▨▨▨▨▨▨ or mailed the requested information to my attention at the address on this letterhead. All correspondences sent to our office regarding this application should include reference number ▨▨▨▨▨.

Your request has been placed in pending until the requested information has been received and reviewed by our office.

Sincerely,

Senior Staff Veterinarian

printed materials but as text and image files on highly designed and branded flash drives, while those from Spain and Singapore were contained on CDs. This would extend, in 2011, to DVDs and webpages. While we could catalog the media devices and their contents, we knew they were inherently unstable. As for the content residing on a pavilion or event website, we assumed it would disappear once the Biennale closed. What had begun as a collection-development project was morphing into ongoing preservation activities.

Thus, we created the Venice Biennale (E-Biennale) Preservation Archive in the library's digital asset management system, where we upload the contents obtained from press kits. Text, image, and (later) audio and video files were stored so they can be viewed by visitors to the library, adding a more tangible dimension to exploring the Biennale from afar. The E-Biennale Preservation Archive began as a handful of files; today it numbers 237. Because we were now spending time on the various websites for national pavilion and collateral events, we took note of the great quantity of digital content available. For example, Christian Boltanski's exhibition *Chance* in the French Pavilion in 2011 included an interactive game in which viewers were challenged to click at the moment when jumbled images of facial features on nine grids line up to create a single face. Boltanski also created a website for the game, inviting global participation. The library set out to capture this as well. The site disappeared before we could, but it prompted yet another development in our collecting activity.

The Clark's former collections management librarian, Penny Baker, thought that there might be a better way to systematically capture these materials, and in the weeks leading up to the 2013 iteration of the Biennale, the library entered into a collaboration with Archive-it, a web archiving service created by the Internet Archive. Library staff would create a list of organizational websites, videos, blogs, and social-media accounts that promised to bring our collection of content relating to the Venice Biennale to a new level. The Archive-it service would "crawl" the sites for the duration of the fair. We call the collection the Venice Biennale on the Web, and because we obtained permission from each content provider, we are able to make this collection readily available. This collection also continues to grow, from ninety-eight archived sites in 2013 to 517 today.

In Venice in 2013, Heneage was also ramping up his game, bringing Olivia Floyer from his London staff. The two traversed the city separately, thus covering more ground than had previously been possible. The bounty they returned included twenty-three posters from the Angolan Pavilion. Writing in the *New York Times*, Holland Cotter, who had accompanied Thomas on at least one of his daily treks, described the scene: "Every now and then, a visit gives a shock. When I climbed the stairs of an old building to the Angola pavilion, I couldn't believe my eyes. Gorgeous photographs by Edson Chagas, from the city of Luanda, were there, in neat stacks of giveaway prints" (fig. 4).[2] From Jasmina Cibic's installation *For our Economy and Culture* in the Slovenian Pavilion, Thomas was able to acquire a roll of the wallpaper that covered the walls with scientific illustrations of a blind beetle discovered in Slovenia in 1933 and bearing the unfortunate name *Anophthalmus hitleri*. The "Hitler beetle" is so sought after as a souvenir that it is close to extinction. Thomas also brought back a souvenir in its own right, a small lapel pin with an image of the beetle and the text "For our Economy and Culture" (fig. 5) as well as the now-ubiquitous tote bag—perhaps the most popular ephemera type at the Biennale.

Tote bags, wallpaper, lapel pins, flash drives, letters denying the import of salami—the collection was certainly stretching the

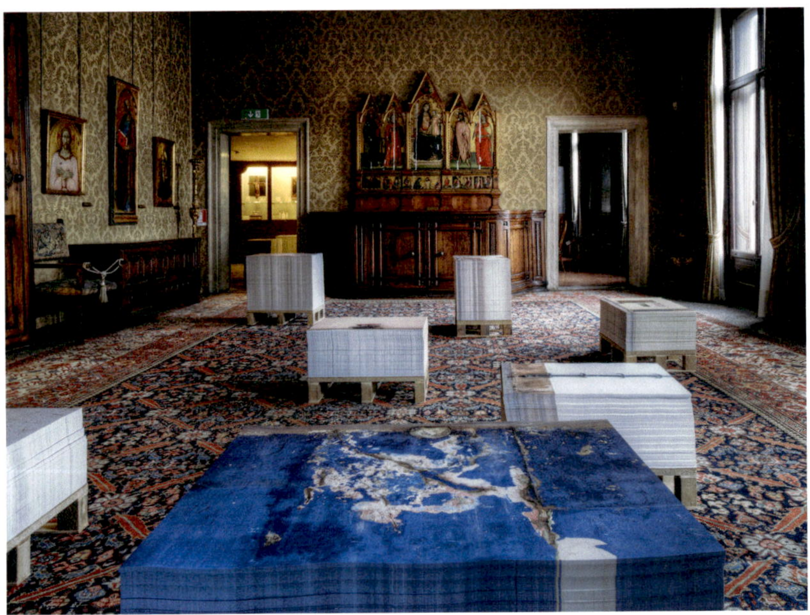

FIG 4 | CAT 1 Edson Chagas (Angolan; b. Luanda, 1977), installation view of *Luanda, Encyclopedic City*, Angolan Pavilion of the 55th Venice Biennale, 2013

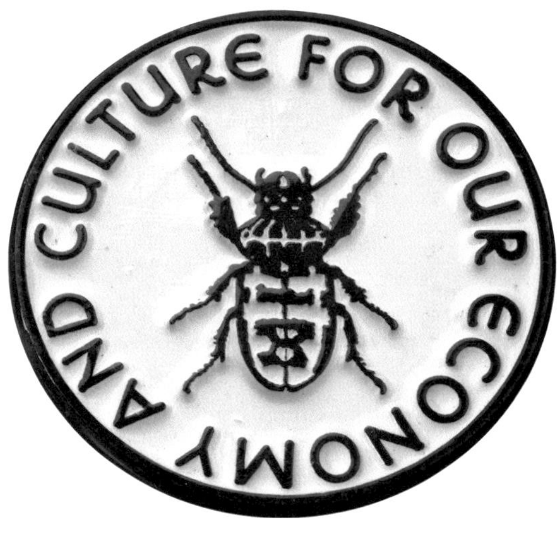

FIG 5 Jasmina Cibic (Slovenian; b. Ljubljana, 1979), lapel pin from *For Our Economy and Culture*, Slovenian Pavilion of the 55th Venice Biennale, 2013. Diameter: 1 in. (2.5 cm). Clark Art Institute Library, Venice Biennale Ephemera Collection

boundaries of material usually found in a research library, and it was becoming difficult to convey the scope of the material in a typical cataloging record. Accordingly, in 2014 the library partnered with the Digital Photography Lab at Boston Public Library to photograph selected items from the collection. We were then able to create a digital collection called the Venice Biennale Ephemera Collection, which debuted in early 2015 with eighty-four object images. It now contains 254 objects and is accessible freely online.

While we intended to restrict our collection-development activities to officially sanctioned exhibitions and events, we are willing to make exceptions. For example, in 2015 we documented the actions of the anonymous Ukranian activist group #ONVACATION, who staged an occupation of the Russian Pavilion. Wearing camouflage jackets embossed on the back with #ONVACATION, they protested Russian claims that soldiers invading Crimea were simply enjoying a vacation. The artists also distributed jackets and tote bags (fig. 6) to the public, encouraging them to similarly occupy pavilions of their choice, take selfies, and post them to social-media sites with the hashtag #ONVACATION. In June, a raffle was held with a prize of a free vacation to the Crimean city of Balaklava. Olivia Floyer, who had joined Thomas again that year, was a willing participant, and the jacket is now in the library's collection.

That same year, we were also lucky to obtain materials related to the Icelandic Pavilion, which was only open for two weeks before being shut down by Venetian authorities. Representing Iceland, the Swiss artist Christoph Büchel had installed his project *THE MOSQUE: The First Mosque in the Historic City of Venice* in the former Catholic church of Santa Maria dell'Abbazia della Misericordia (see fig. 15). Büchel's

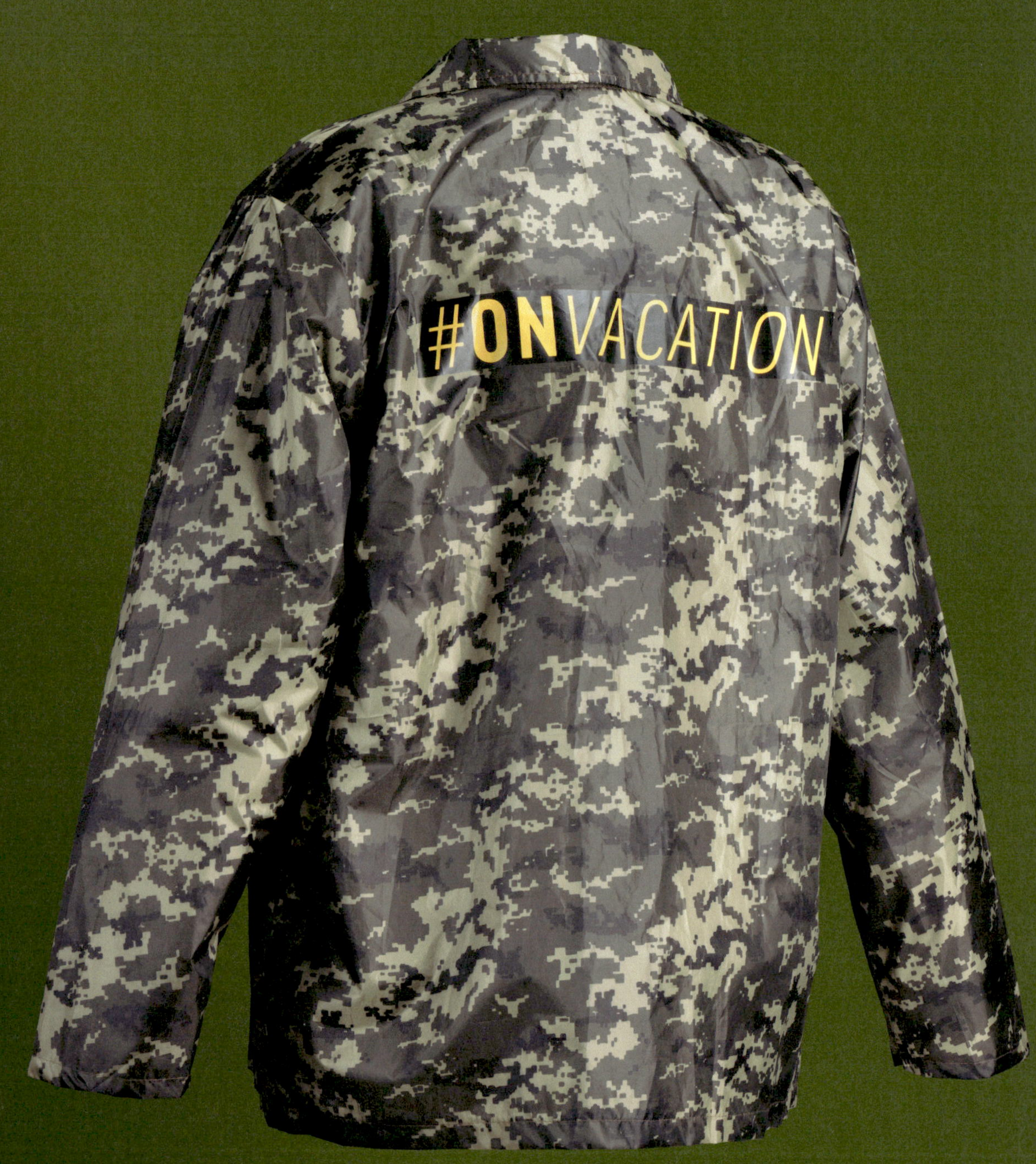

FIG 6 | CAT 86–87 Anonymous artists, jacket and tote bag from *#ONVACATION*, an unsanctioned project from the 56th Venice Biennale, 2015. Jacket: 33 ¼ × 27 ½ in.; sleeve length: 26 ¼ in. (84.5 × 69.9 cm; sleeve length: 66.7 cm); tote bag: 15 ¼ × 13 ⅝ in. (38.7 × 34.6 cm). Clark Art Institute Library, Venice Biennale Ephemera Collection

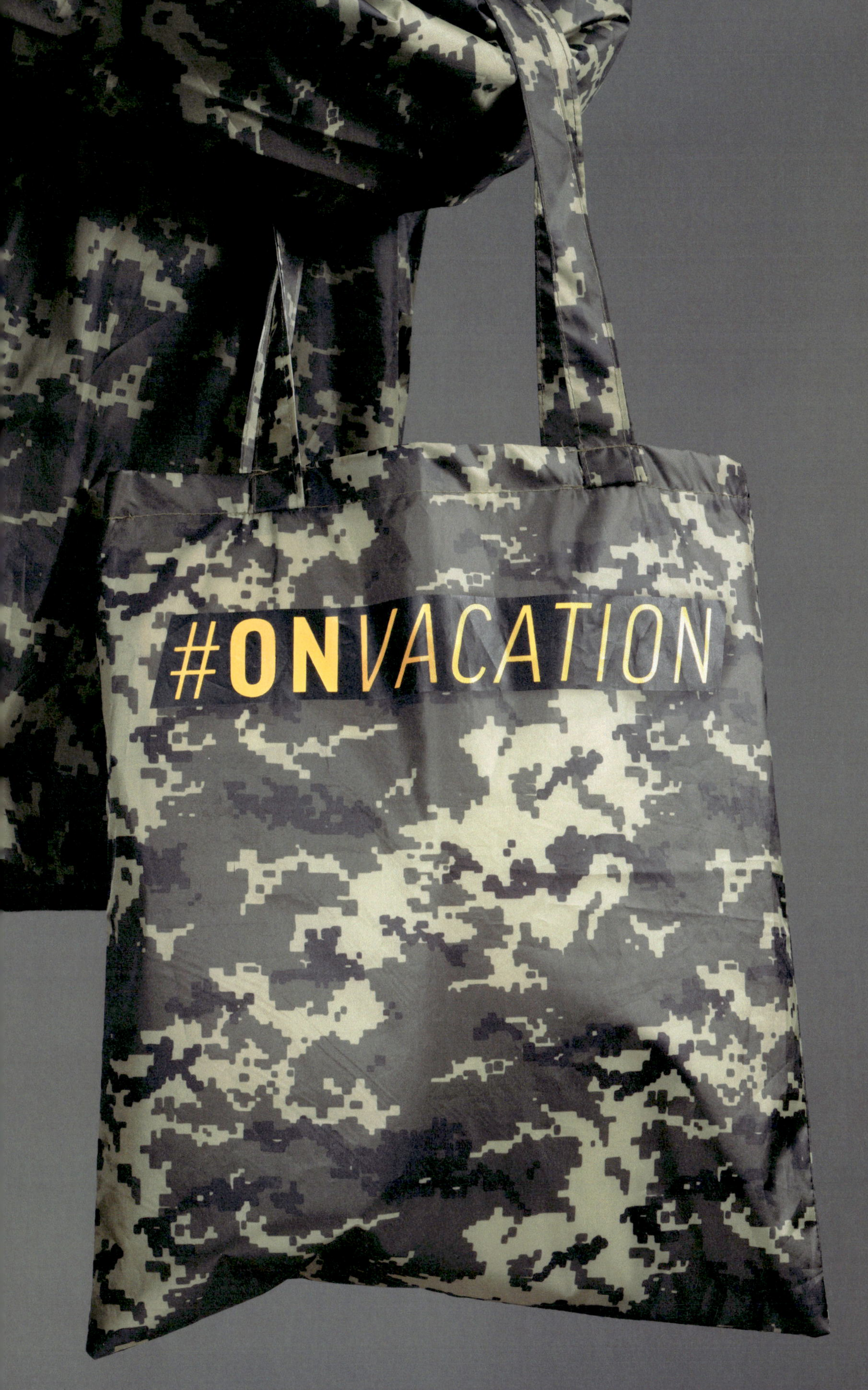

#ONVACATION

THE ABSENCE OF PATHS

>>>>

>>>>

VISA
APPLICATION
FORM

FREESA NUMBER

>>>>

NAME ⌄

SURNAME ⌄

EMAIL ADDRESS ⌄

WHERE DO YOU BELONG? ⌄

CIRCLE HOME ⌄

TUNISIA NATIONAL PAVILION
57TH INTERNATIONAL
ART EXHIBITION –
LA BIENNALE DI VENEZIA

> www.theabsenceofpaths.com

In submitting this form I agree to my details being used to anonymously reference my
chosen home location on the website of 'The Absence of Paths'. The information will only
be accessed by exhibition staff. I understand my data will be held securely and will not
be distributed to third parties. I understand that when this information is no longer
required for this purpose, official procedure will be followed to dispose of my data.

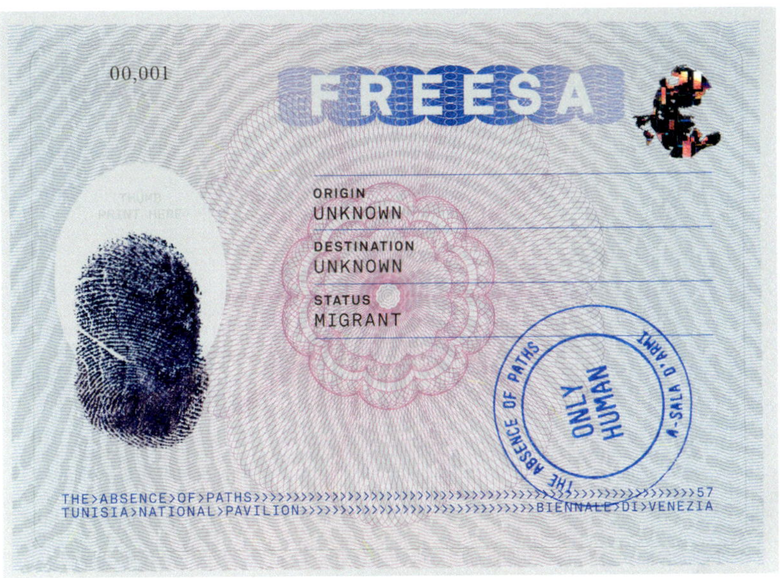

FIG 7 | CAT 82–83 Application (*left*) and Freesa (*above*) from *The Absence of Paths*, Tunisian Pavilion of the 57th Venice Biennale, 2017. Application: 5 ¾ × 3 in. (14.6 × 7.6 cm); booklet: 6 ¾ × 4 in. (17.1 × 10.2 cm). Clark Art Institute Library, Venice Biennale Ephemera Collection

project highlighted both the historical influence of Islamic culture on the city of Venice as well as the contemporary European migrant crisis. Citing a host of issues, including the possibility of a terrorist threat, the police ordered the site closed. Included in the collection of ephemera is a copy of the police order, obtained for us by Randy Kennedy of the *New York Times.*

The ongoing migration crisis was highlighted again in 2017, most notably by the Tunisian Pavilion and the artists' collective Neue Slovenische Kunst (NSK). Tunisia returned to the Biennale after an absence of fifty years, though not with a traditional national pavilion. Instead, its project, *The Absence of Paths*, came in the form of a universal visa, or *freesa*, that visitors could apply for and obtain at one of three kiosks installed across the city. The document, resembling an official passport, identifies each holder as a migrant, a global citizen in a world with no borders (fig. 7). Similarly, NSK brought its ongoing project *NSK State in Time* in the form of an unofficial NSK State Pavilion at the Palazzo Ca' Tron, which included an NSK passport office. NSK has issued passports since 1992 that request "all competent foreign authorities to allow the bearer . . . to pass freely without let or hindrance and to afford the bearer such assistance and protection as may be necessary." The library's collection includes examples of each (fig. 8).

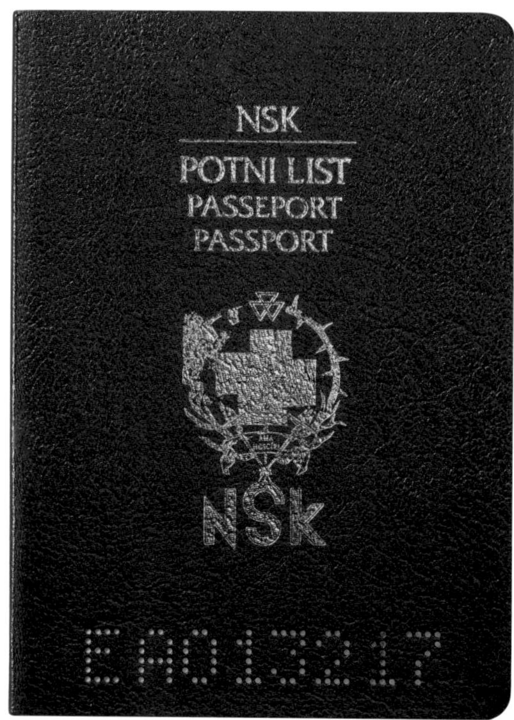

FIG 8 | CAT 89 Passport issued by NSK State, unsanctioned event at the 57th Venice Biennale, 2017. 5 × 3 ½ in. (12.7 × 8.9 cm). Clark Art Institute Library, Venice Biennale Ephemera Collection

Art's Biggest Stage: Collecting the Venice Biennale, 2007–2019 is the first exhibition to dive deep into the library's various holdings related to the event. Drawing primarily from our collection of publications and ephemera, curator Brian Sholis has emphasized notions of nationhood while at the same time evoking the spectacle of the Biennale itself. I hope that the narratives he has uncovered will be the first of many offered by these collections.

1   Randy Kennedy, "Artwork to Display, or to Enjoy With Eggs," *New York Times*, July 3, 2009, www.nytimes.com/2009/07/04/arts/design/04salami.html.

2   Holland Cotter, "Beyond the 'Palace,' an International Tour in One City," *New York Times*, June 6, 2013, www.nytimes.com/2013/06/06/arts/design/venice-biennale-in-its-55th-edition.html.

SUSAN ROEPER

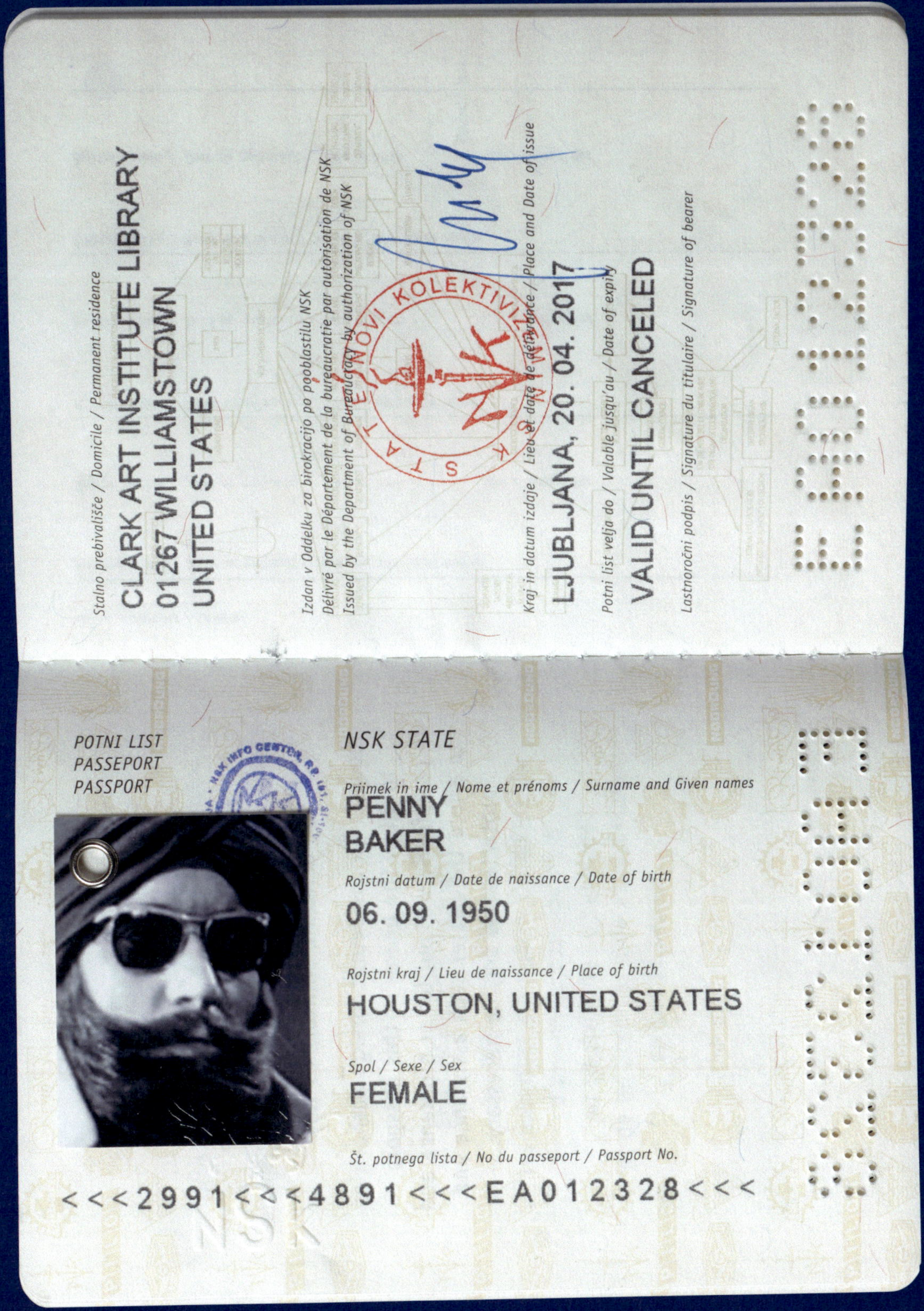

Stalno prebivališče / Domicile / Permanent residence

**CLARK ART INSTITUTE LIBRARY
01267 WILLIAMSTOWN
UNITED STATES**

Izdan v Oddelku za birokracijo po pooblastilu NSK / Délivré par le Département de la bureaucratie par autorisation de NSK / Issued by the Department of Bureaucracy by authorization of NSK

Kraj in datum izdaje / Lieu et date de délivrance / Place and Date of issue

LJUBLJANA, 20. 04. 2017

Potni list velja do / Valable jusqu'au / Date of expiry

VALID UNTIL CANCELED

Lastnoročni podpis / Signature du titulaire / Signature of bearer

---

POTNI LIST
PASSEPORT
PASSPORT

NSK STATE

Priimek in ime / Nome et prénoms / Surname and Given names

**PENNY
BAKER**

Rojstni datum / Date de naissance / Date of birth

06. 09. 1950

Rojstni kraj / Lieu de naissance / Place of birth

HOUSTON, UNITED STATES

Spol / Sexe / Sex

FEMALE

Št. potnega lista / No du passeport / Passport No.

<<<2991<<4891<<<EA012328<<<

CRIMINAL CASE

№ 6 ▮▮▮▮

CRIMINAL CASE
N° 6 ▮▮▮▮

Kaarel,

118 (1)[1]

118 (2)[2]

Juhan OJASTE : aka the Chairman / forty-five years old / former kolkhoz chairman / at the time of the trial employed as a construction worker / secondary education / expelled from the Communist Party / accused

Kalev POST : the Chairman's connection in Viljandi / fifty-eight years old / waiter / sixth grade education / not a Party member / accused

Mart TROSS : Kalev Post's connection / twenty-three years old / kolkhoz worker / sixth grade education / Komsomol[1] member / opened the court case

Aleksei DYMOV : the Chairman's casual connection in Tallinn / thirty years old / senior engineer / higher education unfinished / not a Party member

Sergei BARKOV : the Chairman's casual connection / nineteen years old / transport worker on a sovkhoz / sixth grade education / Komsomol member

Aita OJASTE : the Chairman's wife / forty-seven years old / kolkhoz animal husbandry technician / specialized secondary education / Party member

Oskar PÜVI : police lieutenant / Viljandi precinct investigator / forty-three years old / secondary specialized education / Party member

Villem JÕGI : police sergeant at the Viljandi police department / twenty years old / secondary specialized education / Party member

Vaike VITSUT : forensic medicine specialist / thirty years old / higher education / not a Party member

CONTENTS

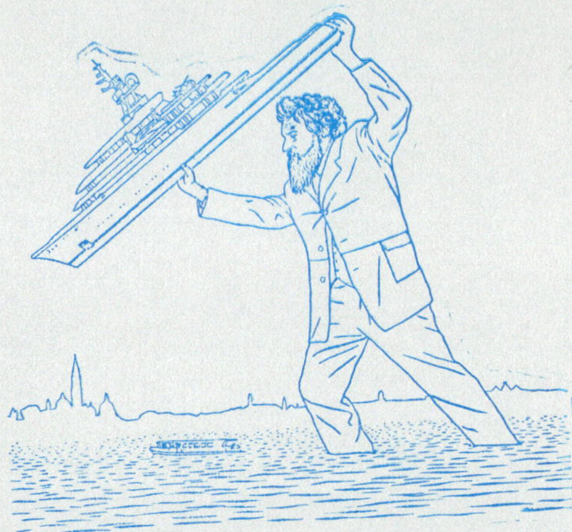

We sit starving amidst our gold
Jeremy Deller, British Pavilion, Venice Biennale 2013

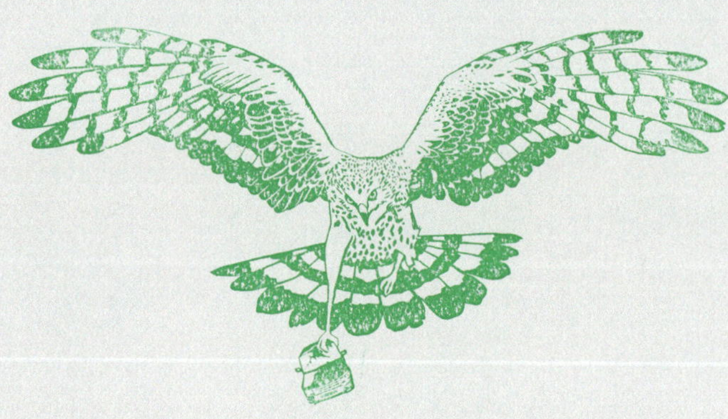

A good day for cyclists
Jeremy Deller, British Pavilion, Venice Biennale 2013

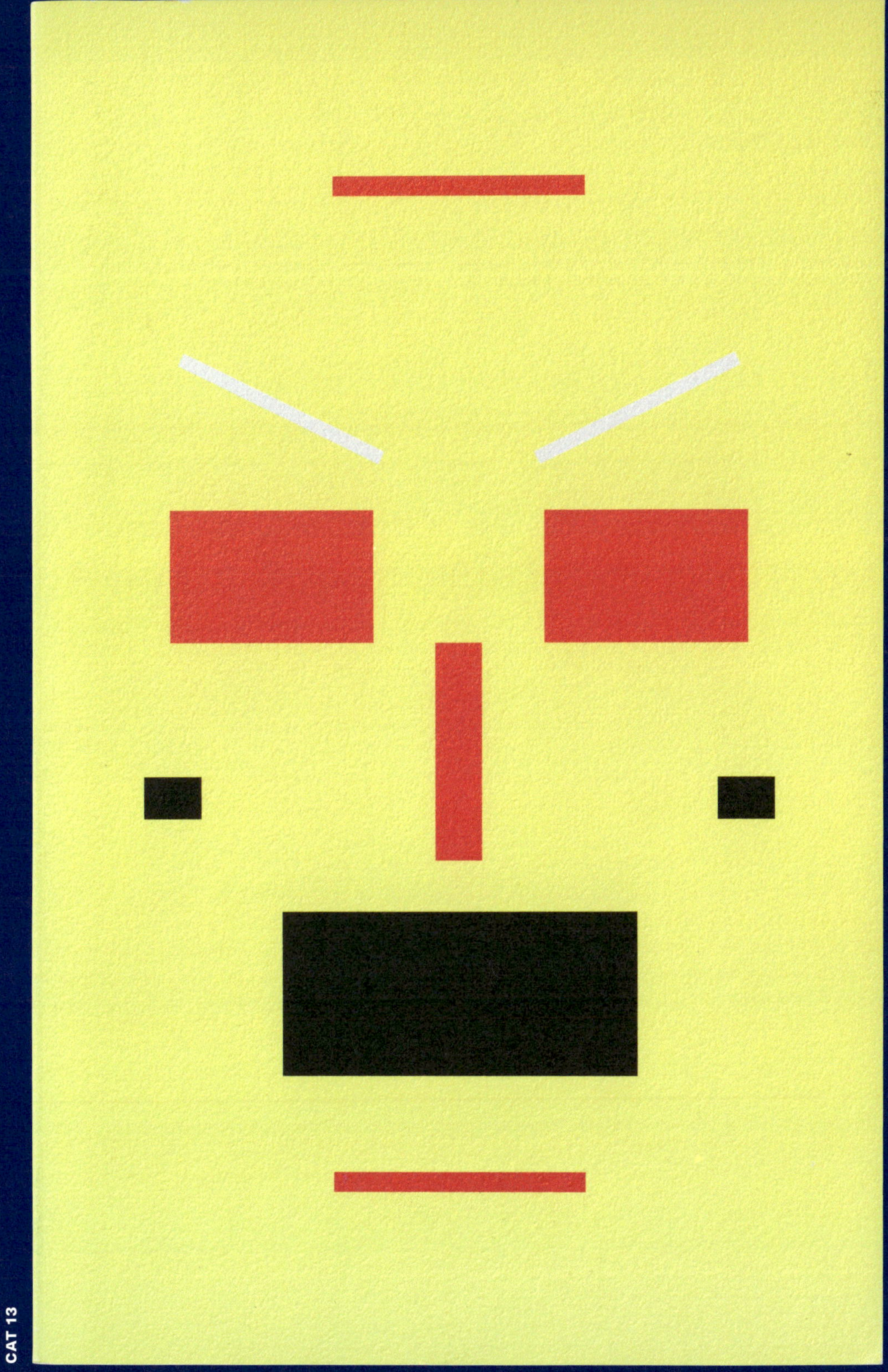

CAT 13

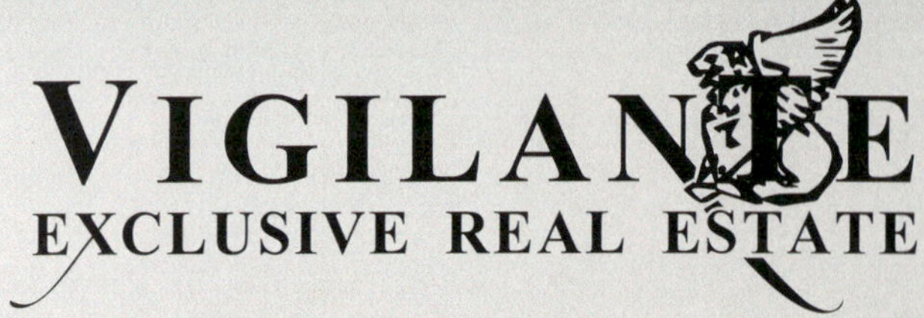

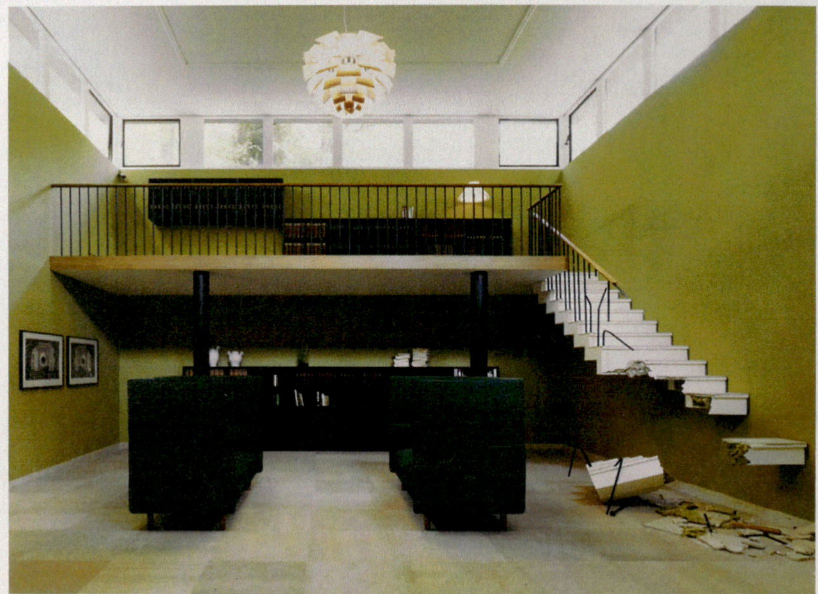

Venice – Giardini della Biennal

Indoor

Cellar

locker room A & B - n.2 toilet- workroom - Gym

Ground Floor

double salon with porch - dining room - live in kitchen with front porch - pantry - laundry - bathroom with gallery and storage - n.1 suite with bathroom and closet - workroom

1st Floor

n.1 double bedroom ensuite with closet and porch n.1 master bedroom ensuite with closet and large porch

Total area: 440m2 + Porticoes

Outdoor

well groomed garden overlooking onto the sea

Total area: 3000 m2

The Encyclopedic Palace has been given an impossible task: no building can contain a universal multiplicity of spaces, possibilities, and objects. When a building tends towards the encyclopedic, it becomes a city. The city includes multiple conditions in the coherence of form—even though this is an urban, conflict-ridden form. Luanda is the privileged research site of the Republic of Angola Pavilion, which continues the curatorial line adumbrated by Beyond Entropy at the 13th International Architecture Exhibition—La Biennale di Venezia. The complexity of Angola's capital, Luanda, derives from the presence of unpredictable spaces and the coexistence of irreconcilable programs: city and country, infrastructure and habitations, garbage tips and public spaces. Luanda is an encyclopedic city. How can the knowledge of a city be organized through the taxonomy of its spaces? Central to the pavilion is a reflection on the ways in which images are used to give form to the way the city is experienced. Edson Chagas's Found not Taken series concentrates on the systematic cataloguing of abandoned objects that are repositioned within an urban context to create new relationships between the objects and their context, form and its codification. What relationship is created between spaces and their images? What role are imagination and creativity allowed to play in this urban taxonomy? In the ambiguity of a vision which uncovers and nonetheless reconstructs, what is delineated is an urban cartography mixing documentary-like precision and poetic reconstruction: a new way of observing the encyclopedic wealth of spaces around us and, perhaps, a new way of inhabiting these spaces.

Beyond Entropy
Paula Nascimento and
Stefano Rabolli Pansera

www.beyondentropy.com

Luanda Encyclopedic City

Pavilion of the Republic of Angola

55th International Art Exhibition La Biennale di Venezia

Twenty-three Offset Print Posters by Edson Chagas

Commissioner
Governo de Angola
Ministério da Cultura

Curators
Beyond Entropy Ltd
Paula Nascimento and
Stefano Rabolli Pansera

Producer
Carlos Major

Graphic Design
Tankboys

Edson Chagas works
Courtesy of
APALAZZOGALLERY

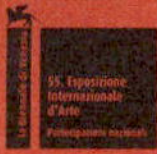

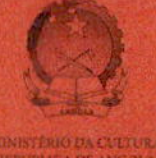

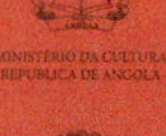

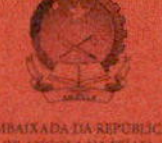

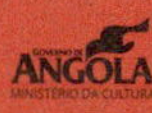

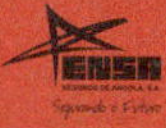

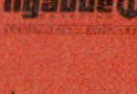

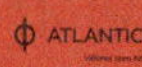

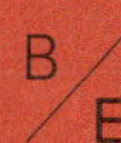

B/E

Beyond Entropy Press

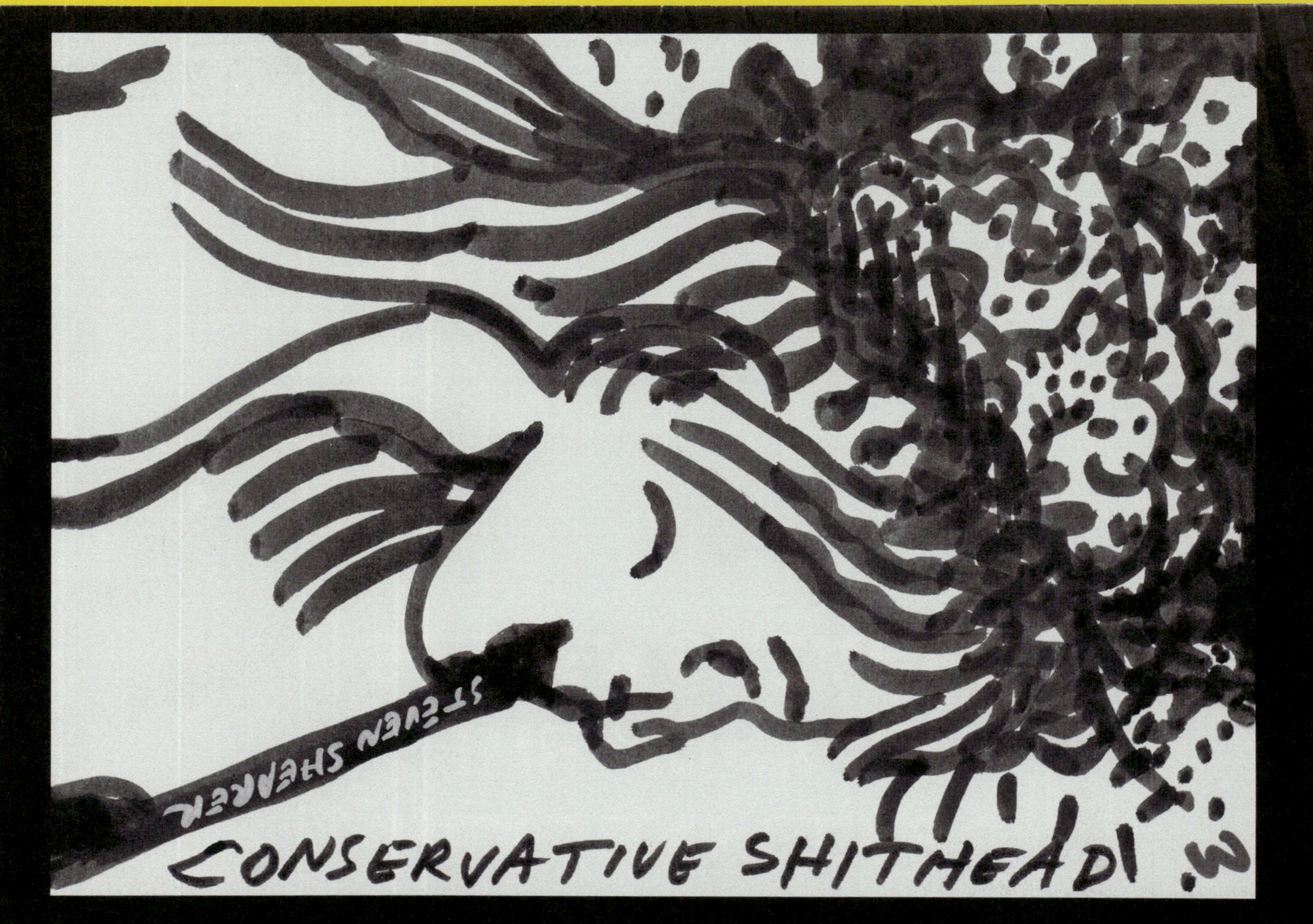
STEVEN SHEARER
CONSERVATIVE SHITHEAD! 3.

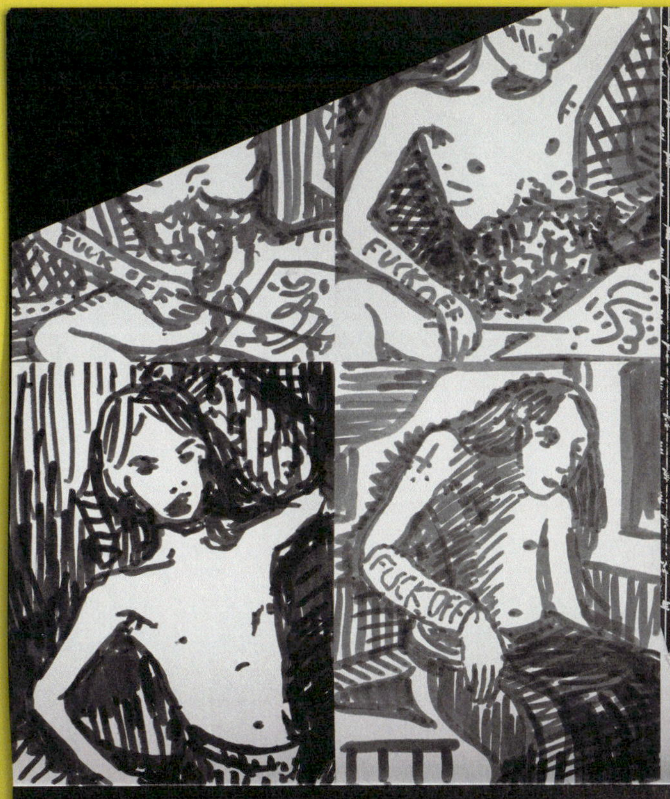

THANKS TO :
*Jérôme Lefevre, Max Loriot, Damien Deroubaix,
Marquis Marky, Dieter Roelstraate, Martin Eric Ain,
Rachelle Sawatsky, Jeremy Hof and Eva Presenhuber,
Markus Rischgasser and Bjorn Alfers from Galerie Eva
Presenhuber, Franco Noero and Pierpaolo Falone from Galleria
Franco Noero, Stuart Shave and Jimi Lee from Stuart Shave/
Modern Art Inc., and Gavin Brown and Bridget Donahue from
Gavin Brown's enterprise*

All images courtesy of Galerie Eva Presenhuber

www.conservativeshithead.com

le-gac-press.com
isbn: 978-2-36409-006-4

C.S. /100

I attended Frères Maristes College as a student but spent most of my weekends with my family in the garden of the Saida Public Secondary School for Boys, which my father founded, near Ain El-Helweh, on the other side of town.

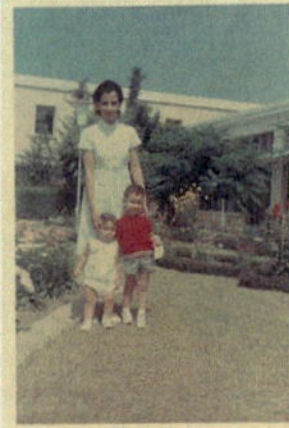
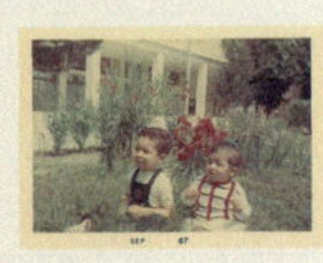
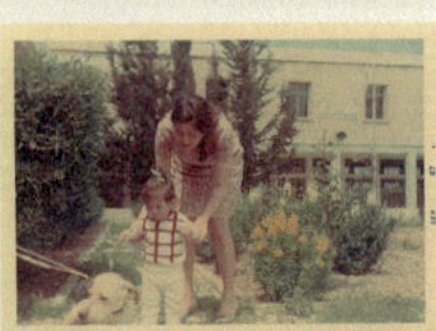
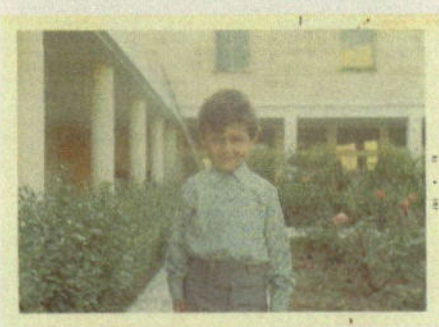

In the late 1960s, the Saida Public Secondary School received yearly gifts from the Ministry of Education, whenever its students excelled on a national level.

In 1970 it received a Schimmel piano. In 1971 it received a sculpture by Lebanese artist Alfred Basbous.

The first art pieces I knew in my life were two.

The first was an oil painting by Hassan Badreddine, who used to teach at the school. It hung on a wall of our home. The second was this sculpture by Alfred Basbous. It was placed in the center of the school's garden.

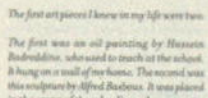
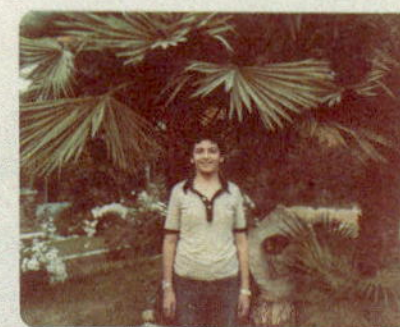
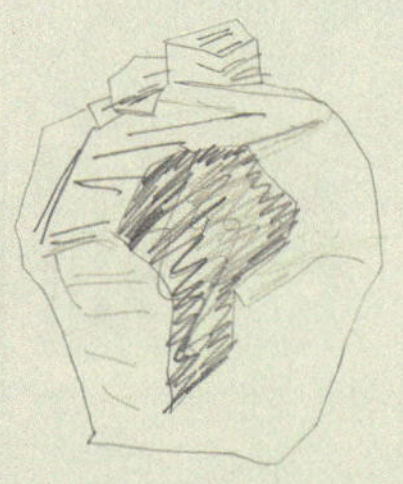

When I was getting ready to move to the secondary level, Saida Secondary School and the Taamir area around it were already becoming a fertile platform for political tensions with Palestinian armed resistance expanding its control outside the refugee camp of Ain El-Helweh.

So I stayed on at Frères Maristes.

Saida Secondary School still serves the community around it in the Taamir district, which overlooks the school playground and, to a lesser degree, the Ain El-Helweh camp a few hundred meters away.

Frères Maristes closed down in 1985 and is now a base for the Lebanese Army.

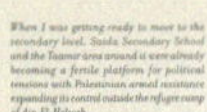
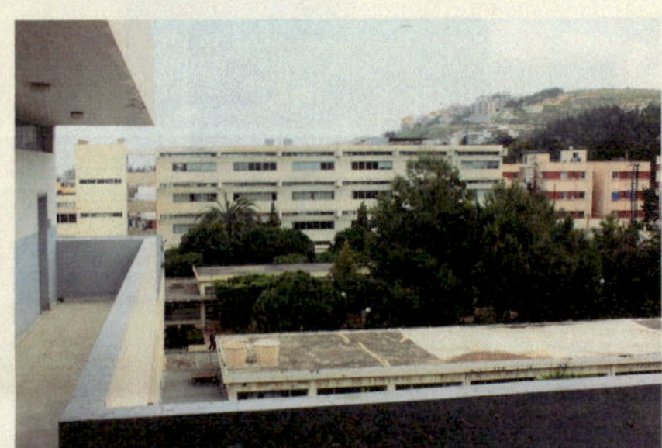
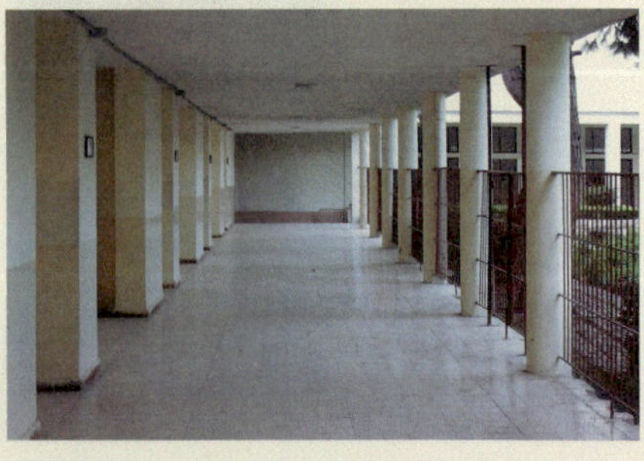
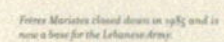
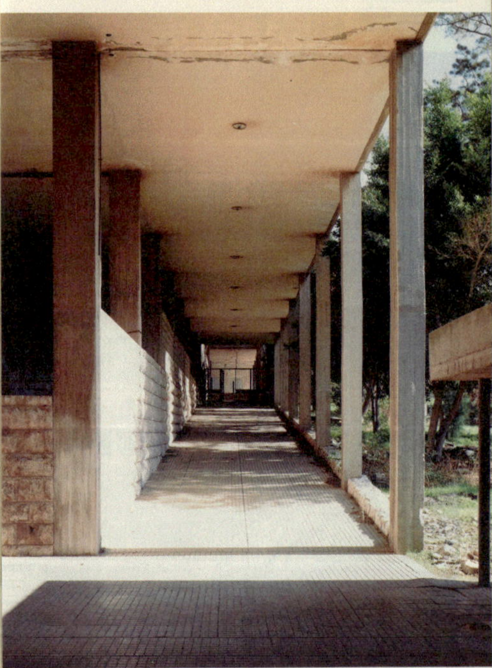

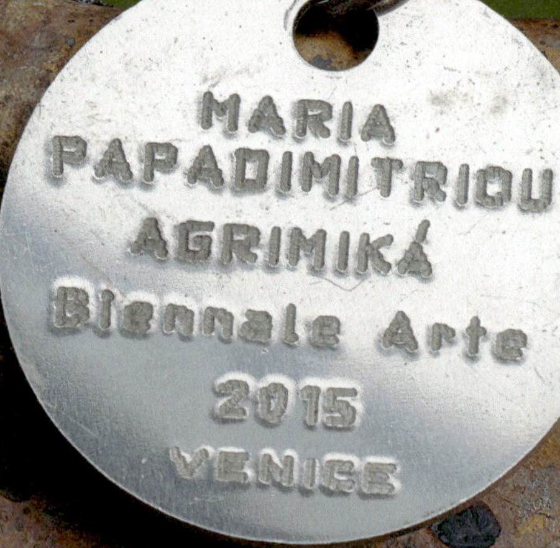
MARIA
PAPADIMITRIOU
AGRIMIKÁ
Biennale Arte
2015
VENICE

International Departures

BRIAN SHOLIS

Every ten years, the Venice Biennale aligns with the timetables of Documenta and Skulptur Projekte Münster, two major recurring exhibitions in Germany. In the summer of 2007, their schedules came together, and enterprising publicists marketed them, somewhat wryly, as being part of a "Grand Tour" that also included the Art Basel art fair.[1] The reference was to the seventeenth- and eighteenth-century custom of upper-class young people, often Britons, touring the continent for months or years to experience art, culture, and the roots of Western civilization. Across two weeks in June 2007, the marketing campaign suggested, contemporary-art enthusiasts could undertake a similar trek, sampling the works of hundreds, or even thousands, of artists in four cities spread across three countries.

A stay in Venice was a highlight for those long-ago travelers, as it "was unlike any other city they visited, whether in terms of topography and architecture, politics and government, or social and sexual mores."[2] Its uniqueness and cultural riches gave Venice a power of attraction that continues to this day. Any encounter with contemporary art at the Venice Biennale can be interspersed with visits to churches and aging palazzi; walks over charming bridges and gondola rides along narrow waterways; and other experiences throughout Venice, which Henry James had in 1892 called "the great museum."[3] By 2007, the Biennale itself had become a big-budget cultural extravaganza that spread throughout the city. As *New York Times* art critic Holland Cotter wrote recently: "The Biennale is as much an archipelago of islands as Venice itself."[4]

It was not always this way. Although the Venice Biennale is the world's longest-running recurring exhibition of contemporary art, and although it serves as a model—to be mimicked or spurned—for hundreds of biennials now taking place across the globe, it assumed its present form only in the last three decades.

The first edition of what became the Venice Biennale took place in 1895. The city had mounted a national exhibition of art in 1887 and, six years later, its mayor, the poet and playwright Riccardo Selvatico, inaugurated a commission to oversee another such cultural celebration. In two years of planning, its commissioners devised a repeating structure and decided to make it an international affair, extending invitations to artists in fourteen countries. They constructed galleries on the grounds of the Giardini, formal gardens created by Napoleon Bonaparte in the early nineteenth century and the site of the 1887 show (fig. 9). The Italian king and queen inaugurated the First International Art Exhibition of the City of Venice on April 30, 1895.[5]

Art historian Caroline Jones has written convincingly that the models for the Venice Biennale were the national exposition and the world's fair, such as London's Great Exhibition of 1851 or the 1889 Exposition Universelle in Paris. As with those predecessors, biennials like the one Venice was launching conduct business and politics—national and international—by other means. "The Biennial came into being as a trade-specific miniature of, *and antidote to*, the exhausted and over-analyzed world's fair," Jones suggests. "The Venetians' future-oriented idea was to focus purely on art, which had long been the easiest mode of exchange within the cosmopolitan trading cultures that nineteenth-century Venice in particular was keen to reinvent."[6]

The 1895 exhibition was a rousing success, drawing more than two hundred thousand visitors. The Biennale would continue, and grow, through the early part of the twentieth century; within a decade, the number of participating artists had nearly doubled. A permanent pavilion for Belgian participation was inaugurated in 1907. Perhaps inspired by the Rue des Nations at the Parisian expositions, Biennale authorities allowed most of the major European states to quickly follow suit, and in the decades since the total number of pavilions in the Giardini has

                                                    BRIAN SHOLIS

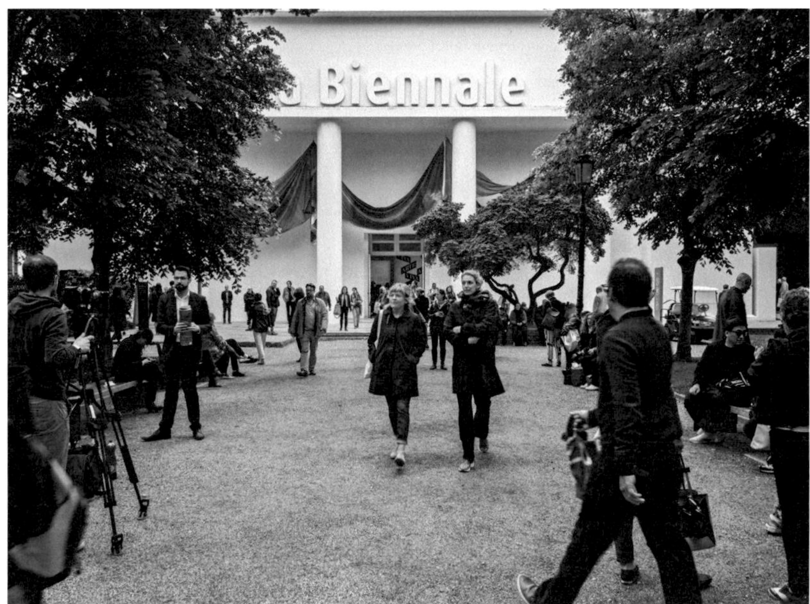

FIG 9 Central Pavilion in the Giardini during the 57th Venice Biennale, 2017

grown to twenty-nine.[7] Under Mussolini, the Biennale passed through a nearly three-decade Fascist phase, with awards for "Best Maternity Subject" and "The Poetry of Labor."[8] A brief hiatus during World War II was followed by a postwar period of cosmopolitan expansiveness. In those mid-century decades, the Venice Biennale model began, haltingly, to be copied around the world. São Paulo, for example, launched its own biennial in 1951.

The changes that give us today's Venice Biennale began in the mid-1970s, when the committee that oversees the exhibition initiated overarching themes for each edition. A decade later, its members began appointing an artistic director from among the increasingly professionalized field of curators prized for their knowledge, their social networks, their management skills, and the number of stamps in their passport. This curator is responsible for a thematic exhibition installed in the Giardini's Central Pavilion (once the Italian Pavilion) and, since the 1990s, in the Arsenale, an adjacent and enormous shipyard complex that had long been used to build Venice's commercial and military fleets.

Choosing the artistic director is the primary exhibition-related decision over which the Biennale's organizing committee has control. The national pavilions are commissioned independently. For example, though organized by a curator and a non-profit arts institution,

American participation is formally commissioned by the Department of State's Federal Advisory Committee on International Exhibitions. (Again, politics by other means.) These pavilions now number more than seventy in each Biennale and have spread beyond the Giardini into rented venues across Venice. Additionally, there are scores of officially sanctioned "collateral projects" likewise dotting the city map. This sprawling collection of exhibitions is what we refer to today when we discuss the Venice Biennale.

Despite how far the Biennale has come in the past century, its organizers' early decisions retain an outsize impact on its current form. As Jones notes of the pavilion structure—and the nation-state politics that underpin it—the Venice Biennale's early twentieth-century committees made "the logical error of populating Napoleon's urban garden . . . with pavilions that fixed spatial relations in a world picture doomed to anachronism."[9]

The Venice Biennale's peculiar structure generates several paradoxes. First, invited artists both represent the commissioning nations and preferably use an internationally recognized visual language to do so. Second, the Biennale's claim to being resolutely "contemporary"— to being forward looking—requires it to be placed in relation to a notion of the past. That past takes at least two forms: the museum, which represents a particular history of collecting and exhibiting artwork; and Venice itself (remember Henry James's quote). Lastly, though so many of the Venice Biennale's artistic experiences respond to their architecturally evocative settings, the Biennale's mandate to renew itself every two years makes it difficult for these experiences to implant themselves in the local community.[10]

The 2007 edition of the Biennale, with which *Art's Biggest Stage* begins, tried to negotiate some of these complications. Its artistic director, the American curator, critic, and educator Robert Storr, endeavoured to redress past oversights by creating an African Pavilion and giving it prominent placement within his allotted exhibition spaces. A jury of experts selected *Check List Luanda Pop*, a show drawn from a Congolese private collection, from among several dozen open-call proposals. The effort was controversial before *Check List* even opened: people argued whether the Biennale should legitimize or aggrandize a private collector's holdings; whether the collector's business and political dealings should bear upon the presentation; whether the artists from outside Africa should be included; and, of course, whether an African Pavilion, representing an entire continent, is an appropriate form of inclusion alongside pavilions devoted to individual countries.[11] "Under-lying the fractiousness was the sense that the very idea of an African Pavilion was impossible, that the very name raised expectations that no single exhibition could begin to fulfill," wrote Kodwo Eshun after the Biennale had opened.[12]

Paradoxically, the exhibition Storr curated, titled *Think with the Senses, Feel with the Mind: Art in the Present Tense*, was criticized for shying away from the contemporary and from politics—or, at best, for not acknowledging the political messages in the art he chose to present. Curator Jessica Morgan noted that the "immaculate Arsenale's tepid, whitewashed neutrality presumably evinces Storr's desire to turn the venue into a 'serious,' museum-like space." She continues: the "middle-of-the-road position that [Storr] has established in Venice . . . makes for such an anodyne exhibition."[13] Or, as art historian Katy Siegel, the exhibition's most perceptive and thorough reviewer, wrote, "the idea that the central issue in art today is the division between head and heart . . . feels tangential to the terribly dark global political situation that much of the work in his show addresses."[14]

Similar criticisms stalked the exhibition organized by Christine Macel, the Biennale's artistic director in 2017. The title of a *New York Times* preview underscored her curatorial emphasis: "A Venice Biennale About Art, with the Politics Muted."[15] Author Rachel Donadio put her skepticism directly to Macel: "In times like these—after 'Brexit' and the election of President Donald J. Trump, with the rise of populism and the return of nationalism . . . can a Biennale curator turn away from politics and focus on art for art's sake?" Macel thought so, and made the case through her exhibition, titled *Viva Arte Viva*. Critics remained doubtful. As writer and artist Chris Wiley noted of Macel's inclusion of works from the 1960s and '70s: "She has cherry-picked the rosier aspects of the countercultural moment while largely avoiding its thornier bits: war, discrimination, sociopolitical strife, madness, death. It's all free love, no Vietnam."[16] Art historian Claire Bishop, in a probing and generous review, noted, of Macel's premise, "it's difficult to let the work talk *and* to articulate an intellectual framework that speaks to the state of the world."[17]

The 2007 and 2017 Biennales represent one end of the spectrum of its artistic directors' concerns and methods. Other recent Biennales reflect different considerations. In choosing the late Okwui Enwezor for 2015, Paolo Baratta, longtime president of the Biennale committee, "wanted a curator for what he called an 'age of anxiety.'"[18] Enwezor's

Biennale was, in some ways, diametrically opposed to Macel's emphasis on art for art's sake two years later. As he asked in the introductory essay to his exhibition catalogue, "Should artists be invited to contribute to the international exhibition merely to present only the mechanisms and internal calculations of their practices? Or can their work, ideas, and concepts infuse the space of the exhibition with a vision of art's relationship to its historical context?"[19] His answers to those questions were a resounding *no* and *yes*, respectively. (One focal point of Enwezor's exhibition was artist Isaac Julien's daily staged readings of Karl Marx's *Kapital*.)

Bishop recognizes the Biennale's varying, almost cyclical, manifestations. Her review of the 2017 Biennale concludes: "For the general audience visiting Venice between May and November, *Viva Arte Viva* is a perfectly strong survey of work largely overlooked by art history and (for the most part) by the market. Those of us seeking more dynamic and catalyzing responses to the end of the world will just have to await the next Biennale."[20]

Her point is also a reminder of the diverging Biennale experiences of art professionals and members of the art-loving public—both the experiences brought to Venice and the experiences of its exhibitions. Professionals who are familiar with many of the exhibiting artists often visit the Venice Biennale during its week of previews, when curators, artists, collectors, dealers, and other members of the art world gather in their thousands, race through the city with detailed itineraries, and trade gossip incessantly. They celebrate the exhibitions and each other at an endless string of breakfasts, canal-side lunches, lavish dinner parties, and after-hours soirées (fig. 10). Those who can't attend follow these goings-on via social media, primarily Instagram, and develop a picture of the Biennale through kaleidoscopic fragments.

There are plenty of parties, but most people attending the Biennale's previews earnestly believe in the power of art and want to understand what they are experiencing. The other component of preview week is a seemingly endless array of talks, panels, symposia, screenings, and performances. Many of the items in the Clark's library collection and exhibited in *Art's Biggest Stage* were collected in this context. Because the Biennale's structure means it is not one exhibition but more than one hundred, the materials that accompany such events are abundant. This trend has accelerated rapidly in the period covered by

 Emily Jacir (Palestinian; b. Bethlehem, 1970), *Stazione*, map and details from *Palestine c/o Venice*, collateral event at the 53rd Venice Biennale, 2009. 20⅛ × 22⅞ in. (51 × 58 cm). Clark Art Institute Library, Venice Biennale Ephemera Collection

the Clark library's Venice Biennale collection. As art historian Jeannine Tang noted in 2007, "The paper trail of a biennial includes not only press material but [also] the discursive media woven into the event: podcasts, blogs, media partners, close relationships with art journals and magazines and their special issues. Exhibitions now pre-produce discourse rather than wait for its post-production, [including] by pro-viding . . . 'platforms' for discussion."[21] Or, as Baratta noted in his pref-ace to the official Biennale catalogue in 2017, "It is as though what has always been our primary work method—encounter and dialogue—has now become the theme of the exhibition."[22]

These conversations, and the art they respond to, often engage issues of personal and national identity, borders, migration, politics, and history. Some of the Venice Biennale's most widely discussed recent projects addressed these themes, occasionally leading to controversy. In 2009, Palestine's first official contribution to the Biennale was an authorized off-site exhibition entitled *Palestine c/o Venice*. For that exhibition, artist Emily Jacir proposed printing the names of vaporetto (water bus) stops along one route through Venice in both Arabic and Italian. The artwork was Jacir's attempt to put the city's public trans-portation system in dialogue with the shared European-Arab heritage of its surroundings. It was approved by all relevant authorities, but, three months before the Biennale opened, the project was shut down abruptly and without explanation. Jacir then created a map and brochure —a guide to an artwork that never existed—that have made their way into the Clark's library collection (fig. 11).

Two years later, Jennifer Allora and Guillermo Calzadilla, artists in Puerto Rico who are partners in life and artmaking, represented the United States. Their exhibition in the American Pavilion, *Gloria*, was marked by the spectacle of a fifty-two-ton military tank turned upside down and topped with a treadmill attached to its treads; an Olympic runner, in Team USA gear, ran on the treadmill for forty-five minutes every day (fig. 12). That same year, in the nearby French Pavilion, artist Christian Boltanski filled its central gallery with a jungle of steel pipes. A long strip of paper, imprinted with anonymous babies' faces, whirred

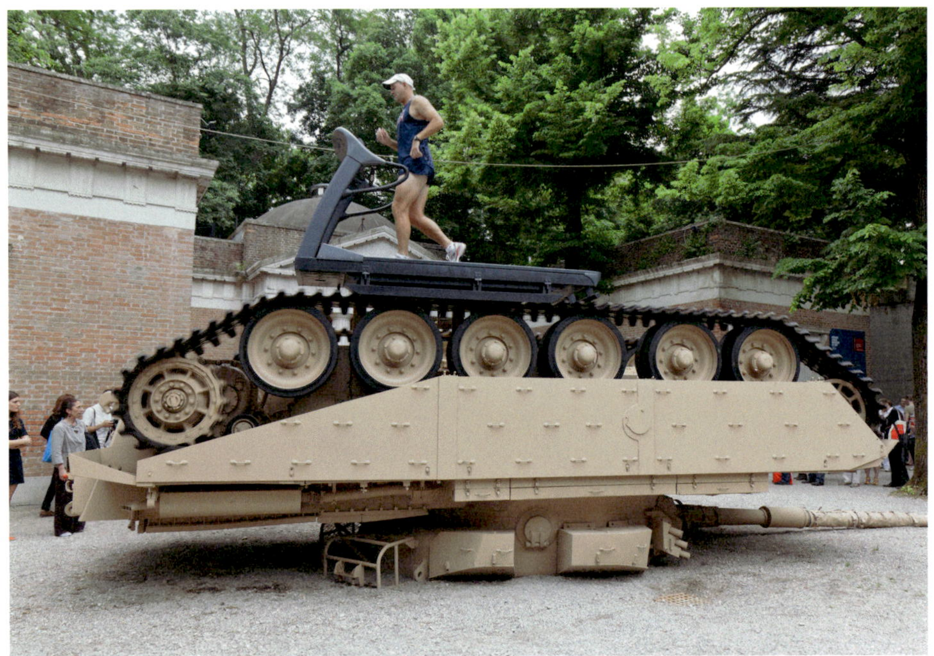

FIG 12 Allora & Calzadilla (Jennifer Allora, American, b. Philadelphia, 1974; Guillermo Calzadilla, Cuban, b. Havana, 1971), installation view of *Track and Field*, United States Pavilion of the 54th Venice Biennale, 2011

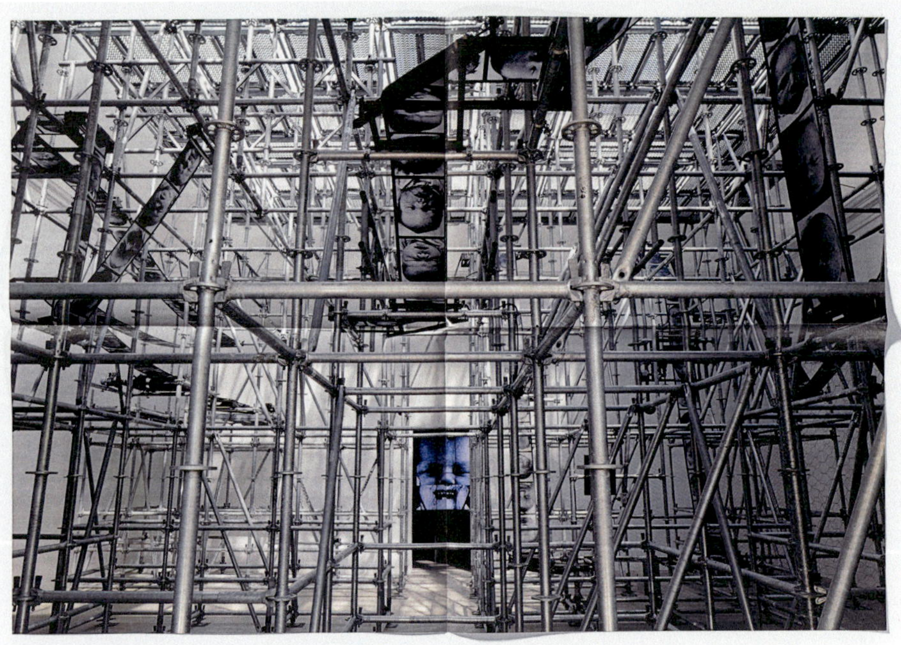

FIG 13 | CAT 29 Christian Boltanski (French; b. Paris, 1944), poster from *Chance*, French Pavilion of the 54th Venice Biennale, 2011. Clark Art Institute Library, Venice Biennale Ephemera Collection

                                                            BRIAN SHOLIS

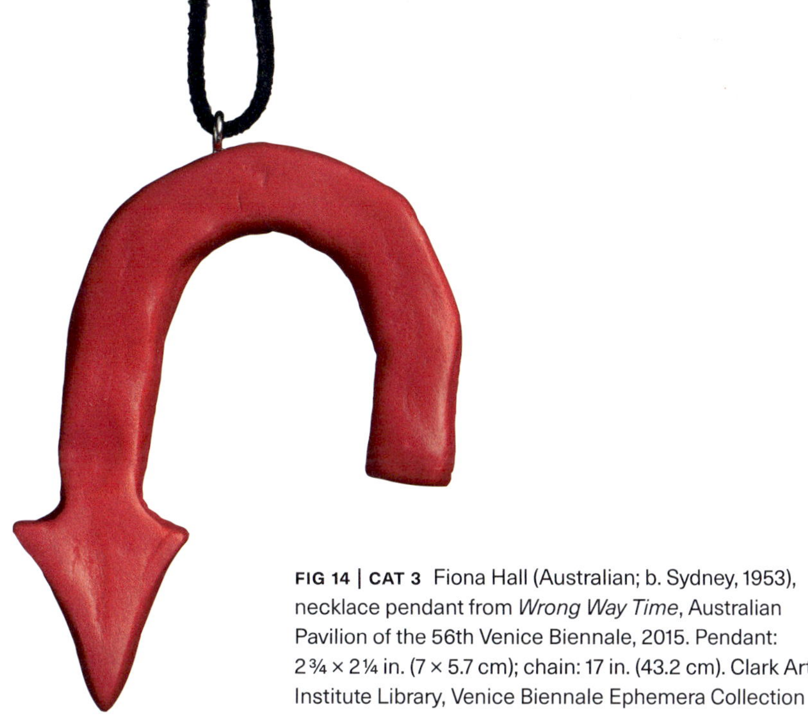

FIG 14 | CAT 3 Fiona Hall (Australian; b. Sydney, 1953), necklace pendant from *Wrong Way Time*, Australian Pavilion of the 56th Venice Biennale, 2015. Pendant: 2 ¾ × 2 ¼ in. (7 × 5.7 cm); chain: 17 in. (43.2 cm). Clark Art Institute Library, Venice Biennale Ephemera Collection

through the installation, stopping intermittently for an alarm to sound and one face to appear on a large screen (fig. 13).

In 2015, Australian artist Fiona Hall inaugurated her country's new pavilion, the Giardini's first new structure in the twenty-first century, which replaced an earlier building. Her presentation of more than eight hundred objects, such as clocks, fantastical camouflaged figures, and international currency, in glassy curiosity cabinets was a sober meditation on global politics, finance, and, above all, environmental degradation (fig. 14). That same year, Swiss artist Christoph Büchel temporarily converted a former Catholic church into a functioning mosque, an endeavour that was shut down by the police after only two weeks (fig. 15).[23] And in 2017, South African artist Candice Breitz presented an hour-long, seven-channel video installation in her country's pavilion that involved actors Alec Baldwin and Julianne Moore reciting the stories of six refugees forced to leave their homelands by persecution, violence, and precarity. In each instance, a social or political message is expressed through a spectacular—or, in Jacir's case, a pervasive—artistic gesture. Each prompts conversation and, after the Biennale, the question, "Did you see *that* in Venice?"

Venice, a relatively small city, appears on the international stage only occasionally. In October 2018, the city's worst floods in a decade brought it briefly into the global consciousness. The images were stark: "Some tourists decided to go for a swim in Saint Mark's Square, in front of the city's cathedral"; "water submerged part of the floor in the

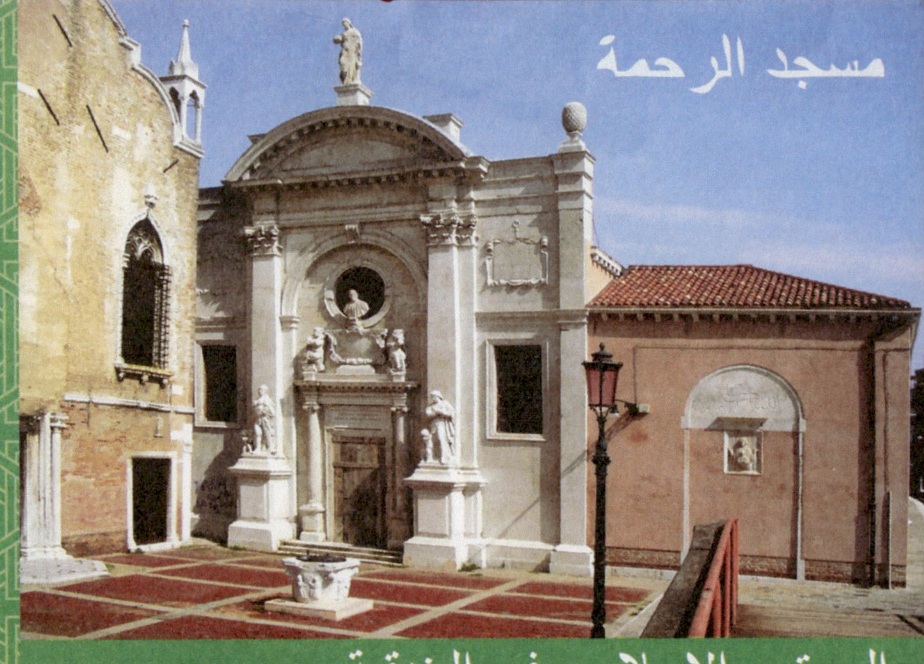

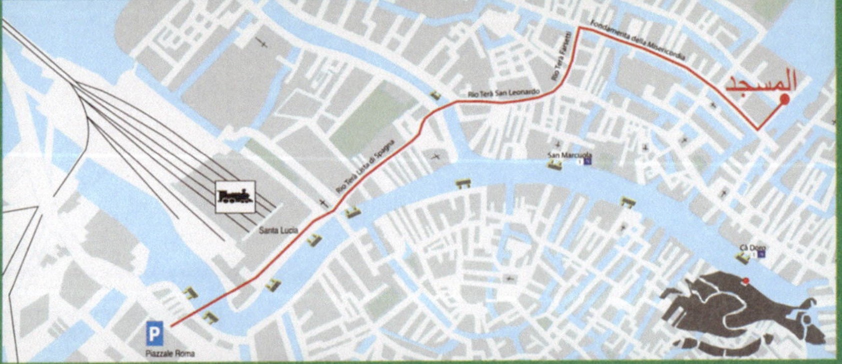

المجتمع الإسلامي في البندقية

La Comunità Islamica di Venezia vi invita a visitare
The Muslim Community of Venice invites you to visit

MOSCHEA DELLA MISERICORDIA

www.mosque.is

أول مسجد في المدينة التاريخية لمدينة البندقية

La prima moschea nella storica città di Venezia
The first mosque in the historic City of Venice

Santa Maria della Misericordia
Campo de l'Abazia
Cannaregio 3548/49
30121 Venezia

سانتا ماريا ديلا ميزيريكورديا
مجال الدير
كاناريغيو 3548/49
30121 البندقية

Friday 8 May - 22 November 2015

الجمعة 8 مايو - 22 نوفمبر 2015

central part of the basilica for only the fifth recorded time in its nine-century history."[24] But the Venice Biennale, ancestor of hundreds of biennials worldwide, makes claims on the world's attention every two years, like clockwork. As the art historian Susanne von Falkenhausen recently observed of biennials: they have become "an important factor in city marketing and in filtering political discourse for a wider public."[25] That is an unexpected pairing. In the Venice Biennale's case, it is a function, on the one hand, of its long and unique history as a recurring exhibition and, on the other, of tendencies in today's art world. It's difficult to know, in light of the city's precariousness and the difficulty of making predictions, in what direction the Biennale will evolve. Those developments, however, will be reflected in the limited-edition artworks, catalogues, and other objects its exhibitors create to share with their audiences—many of which will end up in the Clark's library.

1 An archived version of the Grand Tour 2007 website is available at https://web.archive.org/web /20070329063218/http://www .grandtour2007.com:80/.

2 Rosemary Sweet, *Cities and the Grand Tour: The British in Italy, c. 1690–1820* (New York and Cambridge, England: Cambridge University Press, 2012), 199. See also Bruce Redford, *Venice and the Grand Tour* (New Haven and London: Yale University Press, 1996), and John Eglin, *Venice Transfigured: The Myth of Venice in British Culture, 1660–1797* (London: Palgrave Macmillan, 2001).

3 Henry James, "The Grand Canal," reprinted in *Collected Travel Writings: The Continent* (New York: Library of America, 1993), 315.

4 Holland Cotter, "Beyond the 'Palace,' an International Tour in One City," *New York Times*, June 6, 2013, C1, https://www.nytimes.com/2013/06/06 /arts/design/venice-biennale-in-its -55th-edition.html.

5 For a brisk summary of the history of the Venice Biennale, see Tim Smith-Laing, "The City and the Shadow," *Frieze* 187 (May 2017), https://frieze .com/article/city-and-shadow.

6 Caroline Jones, "Biennial Culture: A Longer History," in *The Biennial Reader*, ed. Elena Filipovic, Marieke van Hal, and Solveig Øvstebø (Bergen, Norway and Berlin: Hatje Cantz, 2010), 72. A version of this article is chapter three of Jones's *The Global Work of Art: World's Fairs, Biennials, and the Aesthetics of Experience* (Chicago: University of Chicago Press, 2017).

7 For more on the architecture of the twenty-nine national pavilions located in the Giardini, see Diener & Diener Architects with Gabriele Basilico, eds., *Common Pavilions: The National Pavilions in the Giardini of the Venice Biennale in Essays and Photographs* (Zurich: Scheidegger & Spiess, 2013). The essays are also available online at http://commonpavilions.com.

8 Smith-Laing, "The City and the Shadow."

9 Jones, "Biennial Culture," 78.

10 This passage draws on Jones, "Biennial Culture," especially pp. 73–74.

11 See, for example, Ben Davis, "Art and Corruption in Venice," *Artnet News*, February 23, 2007, http://www.artnet.com/magazineus/news/artnetnews/artnetnews2-23-07.asp, and Walter Robinson, "Update on Dokolo in Venice," *Artnet News*, May 18, 2007, http://www.artnet.com/magazineus/news/artnetnews/artnetnews5-18-07.asp.

12 Kodwo Eshun, "The African Pavilion," *Frieze* 109 (September 2007), https://frieze.com/article/african-pavilion.

13 Jessica Morgan, "Venice," *Artforum* 46, no. 1 (September 2007), https://www.artforum.com/print/200707/jessica-morgan-42127.

14 Katy Siegel, "Venice," *Artforum* 46, no. 1 (September 2007), https://www.artforum.com/print/200707/katy-siegel-15676.

15 Rachel Donadio, "A Venice Biennale About Art, with the Politics Muted," *New York Times*, May 7, 2017, C1, https://www.nytimes.com/2017/05/07/arts/design/a-venice-biennale-about-art-with-the-politics-muted.html.

16 Chris Wiley, "The 57th Venice Biennale," *Frieze* 189 (September 2017), https://frieze.com/article/57th-venice-biennale-0.

17 Claire Bishop, "The Long View," *Artforum* 56, no. 1 (September 2017), https://www.artforum.com/print/201707/claire-bishop-on-the-57th-venice-biennale-70463.

18 Donadio, "A Venice Biennale about Art."

19 Okwui Enwezor, "The State of Things," *All the World's Futures: 56th International Art Exhibition* (Venice and New York: La Biennale di Venezia and Rizzoli, 2015), 18.

20 Bishop, "The Long View."

21 Jeannine Tang, "Of Biennials and Biennalists," *Theory, Culture & Society* 24, nos. 7–8 (2007): 255, https://doi.org/10.1177%2F0263276407084709.

22 Paolo Baratta, "Introduction," *Viva Arte Viva: Biennale Arte 2017* (Venice and New York: La Biennale di Venezia and Rizzoli, 2017), 14.

23 Journalist Randy Kennedy followed the story in the *New York Times*: "Moque Installed at Venice Biennale Tests City's Tolerance," May 7, 2015, https://www.nytimes.com/2015/05/07/arts/design/mosque-installed-at-venice-biennale-tests-citys-tolerance.html; "Officials Threaten to Close Mosque Installation at Venice Biennale," May 8, 2015, https://www.nytimes.com/2015/05/09/arts/design/officials-in-venice-challenge-mosque

-installation-at-biennale.html; and
"Police Shut Down Mosque Installation
at Venice Biennale," May 22, 2015,
https://www.nytimes.com/2015/05
/23/arts/design/police-shut-down
-mosque-installation-at-venice
-biennale.html.

24 Elisabetta Povoledo, "Venice
Flooding Is Worst in a Decade; Severe
Weather in Italy Kills at Least 11," *New
York Times*, October 31, 2018, A6,
https://www.nytimes.com/2018/10/30
/world/europe/venice-floods-italy.html.

25 Suzanne von Falkenhausen, "Are
Today's Art Biennials Facing an
Impasse?" *Frieze*, August 24, 2018,
https://frieze.com/article/are
-todays-art-biennials-facing-impasse.

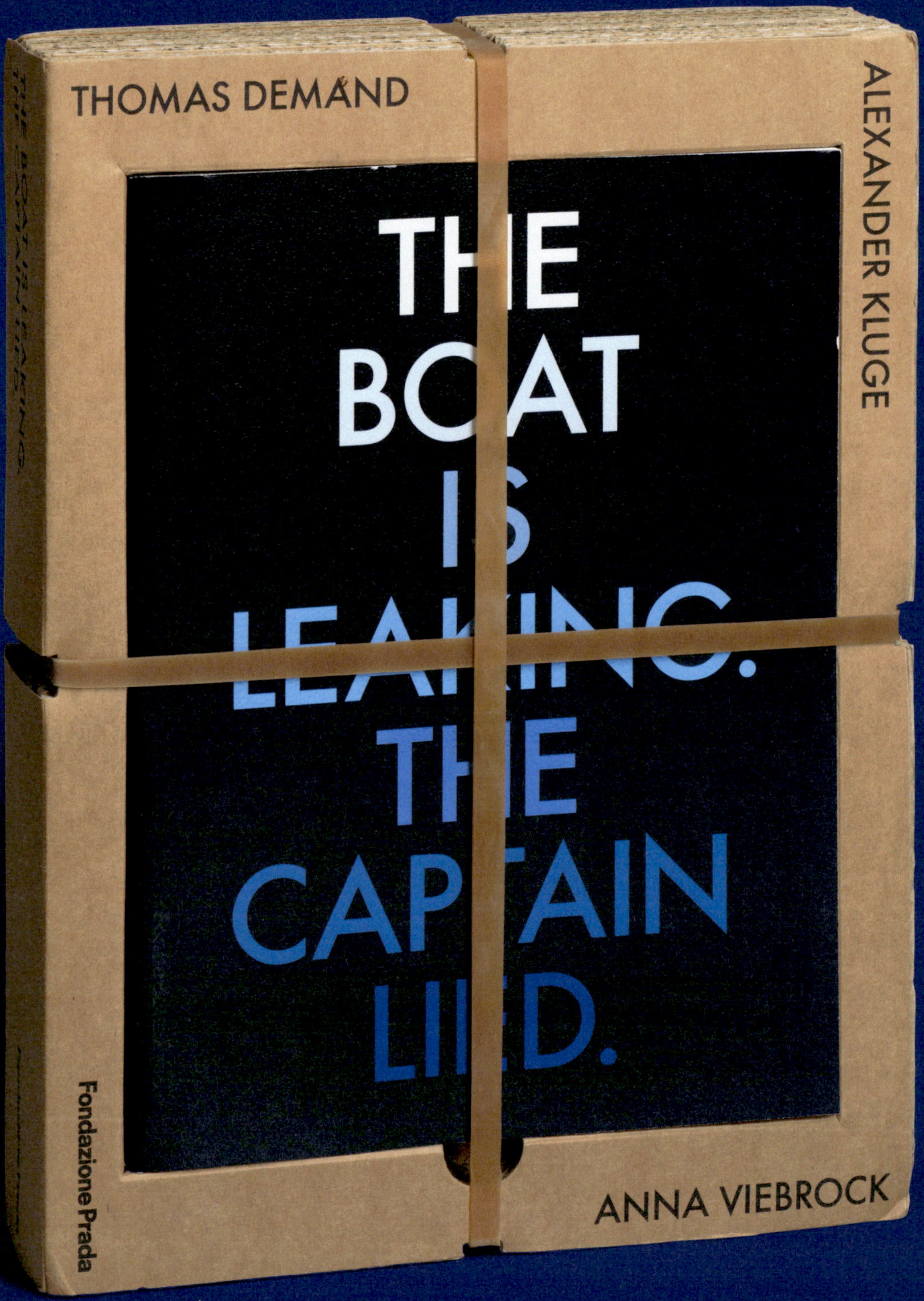

THOMAS DEMAND

ALEXANDER KLUGE

THE
BOAT
IS
LEAKING.
THE
CAPTAIN
LIED.

Fondazione Prada

ANNA VIEBROCK

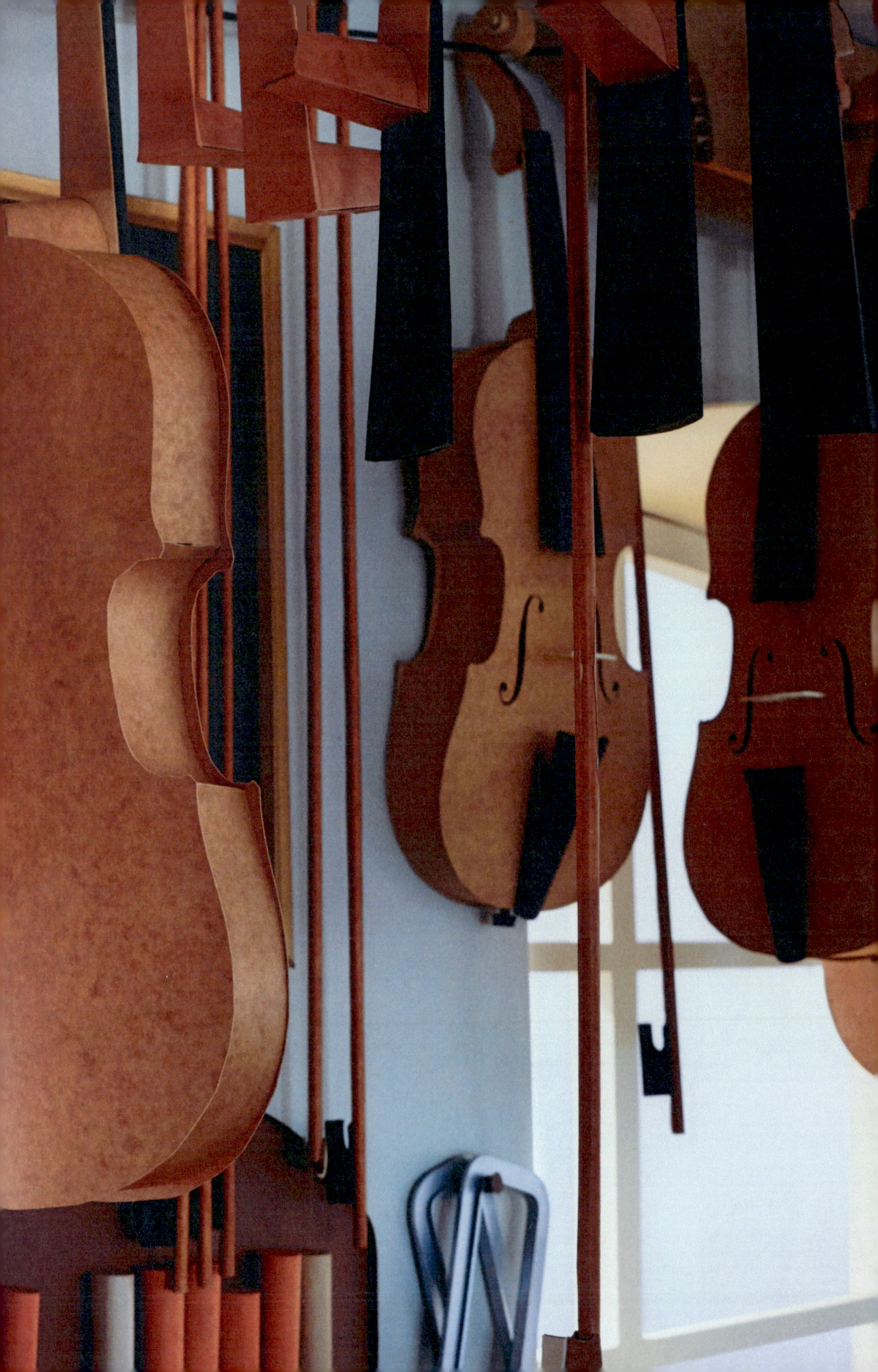

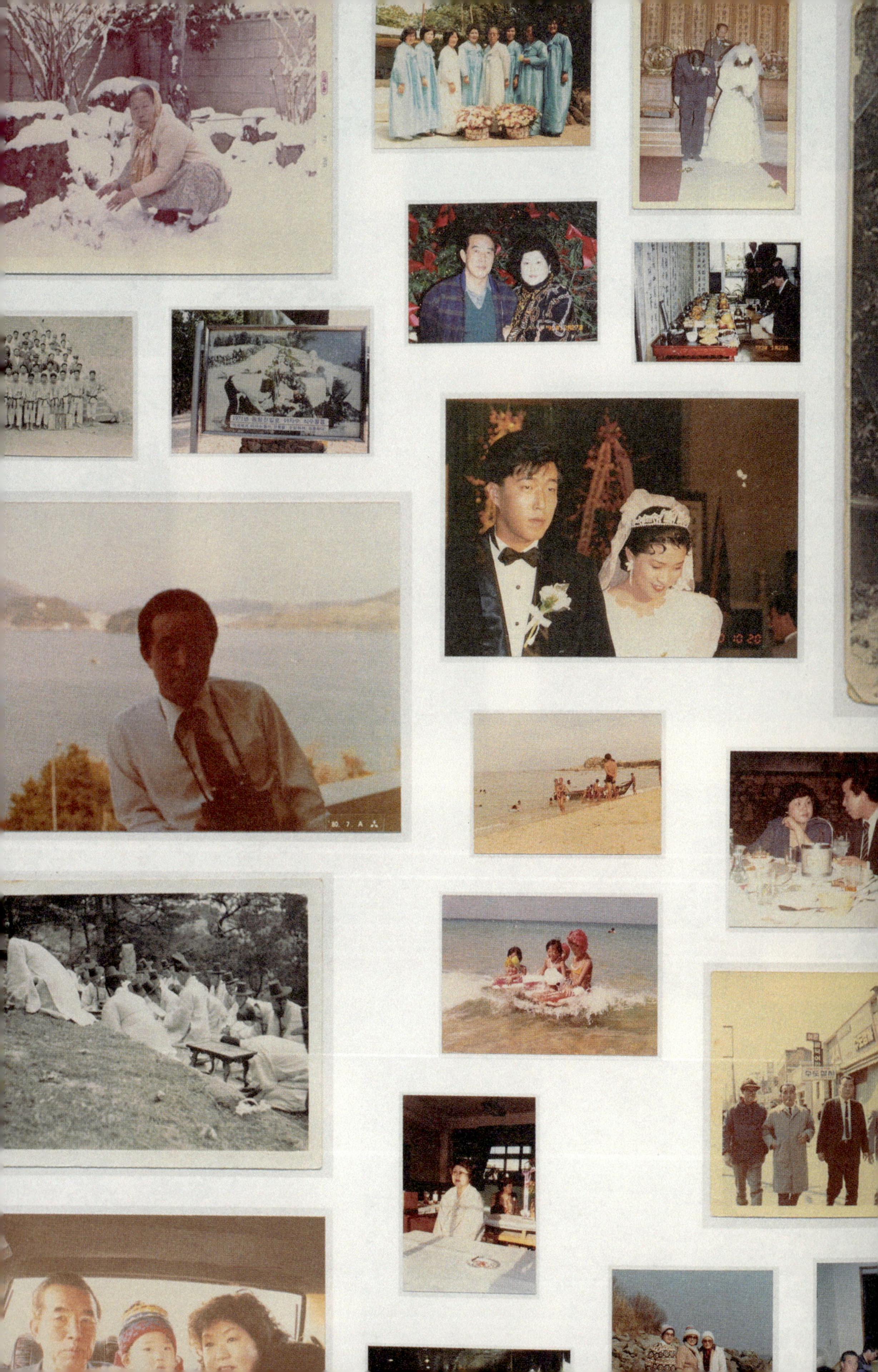

INTERNATIONAL ART BIENNALE
VENETIAN RHAPSODY
THE POWER OF BLUFF
la Biennale di Venezia
57. Esposizione Internazionale d'Arte
KOREAN PAVILION: CODY CHOI

Nathaniel Mellors & Erkka Nissinen

INT. CORRIDOR

Atum faces down the 3 SECURITY GUARDS IN FRONT OF THE
WALL with the BUILDERS STUCK IN IT. A SPED-UP REPLAY OF
THE PREVIOUS SCENE, Atum's LASER BEAM DECAPITATES
THEM ALL MID-SPEAK...

> SECURITY OFFICER 1
> Please don't... I'm young-uh!

> SECURITY OFFICER 2
> Please no kill my wife-uh!

> SECURITY OFFICER 3
> Please don't kill me, I only just parked my car-uh!!

Atum faces the 4th WALL WITH EMBEDDED BUILDERS.

> BUILDERS
> Ignore us, we're just the 4th wall.

INT. SECURITY OFFICE

> THE PRESIDENT
> Builders, you're fired! Security, you're fired too.

We see the GUARD'S DECAPITATED HEADS rolling in the corridor.

INT. CORRIDOR

Atum SMASHES THROUGH the 4th WALL sending
BUILDERS FLYING.
He walks into mist.

INT. SECURITY OFFICE

> TECHNICIAN
> He's broken out. Virtuality levels at zero.
> He's entering the EXTERIOR.

> TECHNICIAN 2
> Son of God entering Original Original Finland.

> THE PRESIDENT
> This was never meant to happen.

<u>END OF ACT TWO</u>

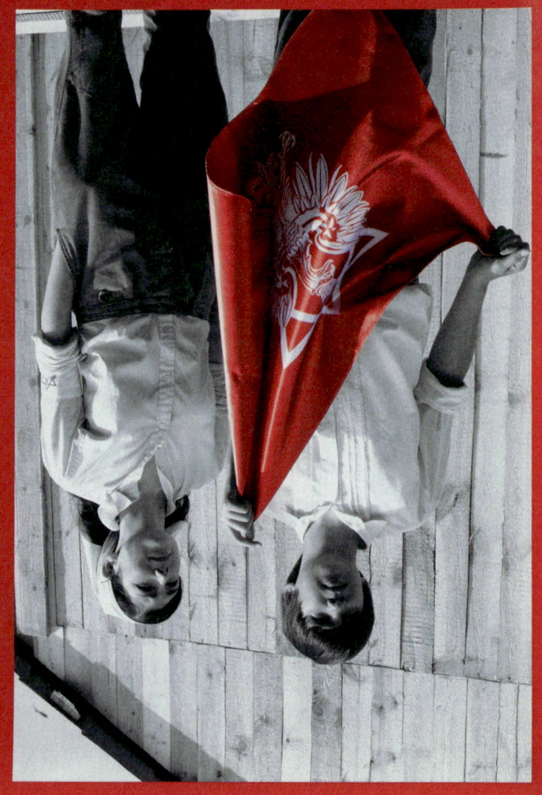

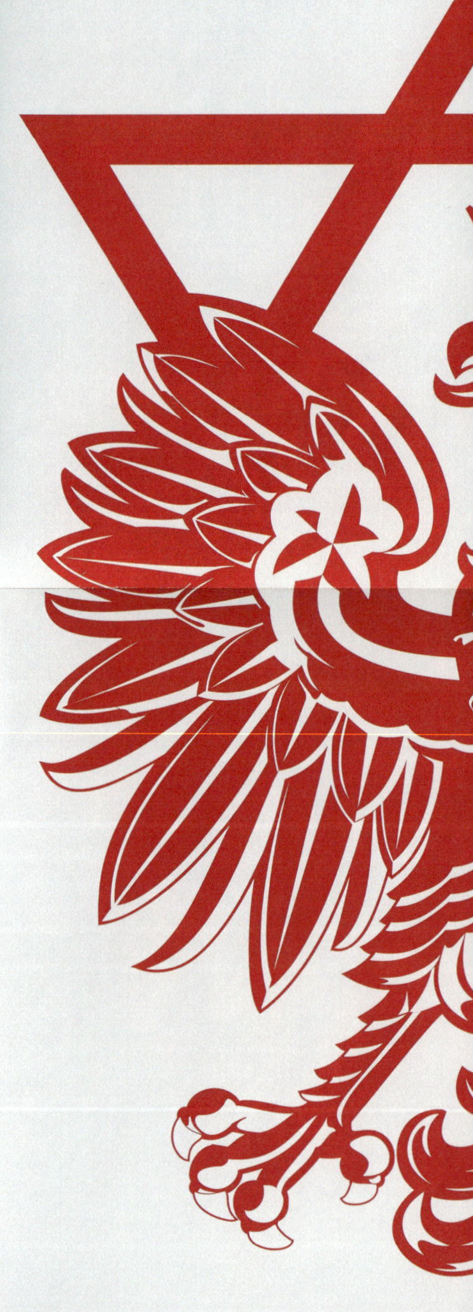

JRMIP CONGRESS IN BERLIN

We want you to join us and take part in the first congress of the JRMiP taking place in Berlin in Summer 2012. For the first time, the members of the movement will gather with international speakers to reflect upon the movement from various points of view. We will discuss the present and the past, our responsibility and our wishes, political and »ordinary« life – and our common interests and particular demands. We will forgive what should be forgiven and create a plan for the future. In fact, we will create our future.

The congress will have three parallel sections entitled *Ideas*, *Entertainment* and *Chill Out*. In each section, guest thinkers and artists are invited to raise and discuss crucial questions operating within the movement to which all participants may respond and look for answers. Films, performances, music and happenings will help us understand and experience our ideas and thoughts more deeply. An atmosphere of chill out will facilitate private conversations relating more intimately to our issue: Jewish Renaissance – not only in Poland, but also in Europe. It will be great to see all of you in Berlin!

The exact days and location of the congress will be confirmed closer to the time and date.

The Berlin Office of the JRMiP will be opened in Auguststr. 69, 10117 Berlin.

The congress will be part of the 7th Berlin Biennale (April 28 to July 1, 2012). The Berlin Biennale is organized by KW Institute for Contemporary Art and funded by the Kulturstiftung des Bundes (German Federal Cultural Foundation).

JRMIP THE JEWISH RENAISSANCE MOVEMENT IN POLAND

The Jewish Renaissance Movement in Poland (JRMiP) calls for the return of 3,300,000 Jews to Poland to re-establish the decimated community. The movement was initiated by Israeli-Dutch artist Yael Bartana in 2007 and has since spread internationally. The aim of the movement is to create an atmosphere for a Jewish reappearance in Poland as well as in Europe. Even if the comeback will be mostly symbolic, at least in the beginning – first steps have to be made. Jews today are not the same people who were expelled from Europe – Europeans today are not the same people responsible for that ethnic cleansing. This is a good time to unite again – to change Europe and Israel for the better (maybe we can change the whole Middle East). Our movement needs all of you who sympathize with such ideas, or whose interests could be represented by the movement. In our manifesto we state:

JRMiP is the response we propose for these times of crisis, when faith has been exhausted and old utopias have failed. Optimism is dying out. The promised paradise has been privatized. The Kibbutz apples and watermelons are no longer ripe. We direct our appeal not only to Jews. We accept into our ranks all those for whom there is no place in their homelands – the expelled and the persecuted. There will be no discrimination in our movement. We shall not ask about your life stories, check your residence cards or question your refugee status. We shall be strong in our weakness.

WWW.JRMIP.ORG

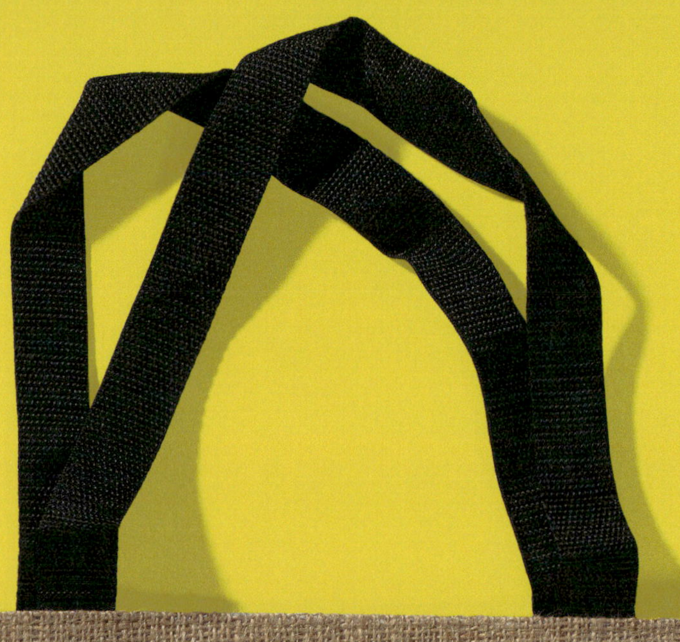

TAVARES STRACHAN
POLAR ECLIPSE
THE BAHAMAS NATIONAL PAVILION
55. Esposizione
Internazionale
d'Arte
Partecipazioni nazionali

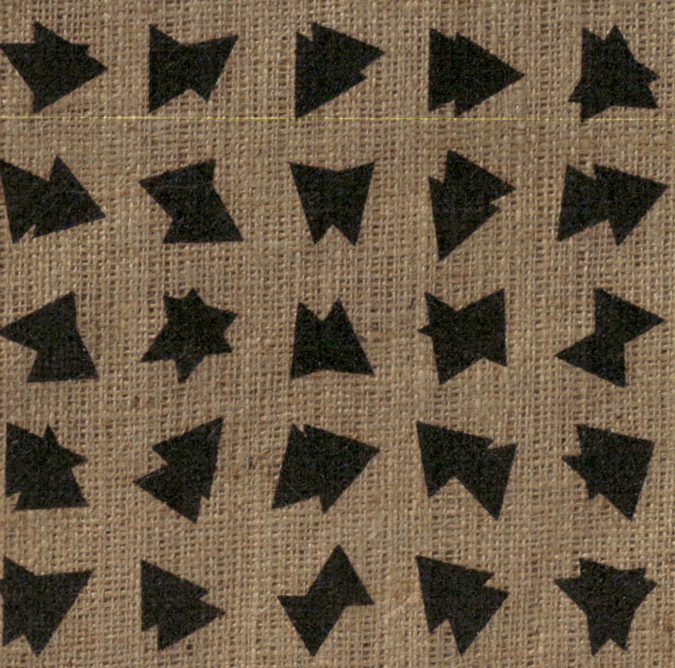

Archiving the Now

SARAH HAMERMAN

As the title *Art's Biggest Stage* implies, the Venice Biennale plays an outsize material and symbolic role in negotiating contemporary art's position within expanding global networks of capital, spectacle, and political power. Launched in 1895, the Venice Biennale is the prototype for a growing contemporary biennial industry that now spans nearly every continent. These complex and often polarizing exhibitions have sparked debates about globalization and postcolonial perspectives in art, the relationship between site-specific installations and tourism, the rise of the curator-as-celebrity, and other key art historical issues. But unlike the museum, another cultural form with roots in the nineteenth century, the Venice Biennale is not a memory institution. Taking place every other year for just a few months, the Venice Biennale is both a temporary and ephemeral event and a perennial attempt to define "the contemporary" as an object to be experienced. Thus, the Clark's Venice Biennale archive can be understood broadly as an archive of the contemporary sedimented in time.

How does the act of archiving shape the narratives that we can draw from the multitude of voices and constituencies embodied in the Biennale's recent history? *Art's Biggest Stage* exemplifies a growing curatorial interest in archival collections not just as raw materials for

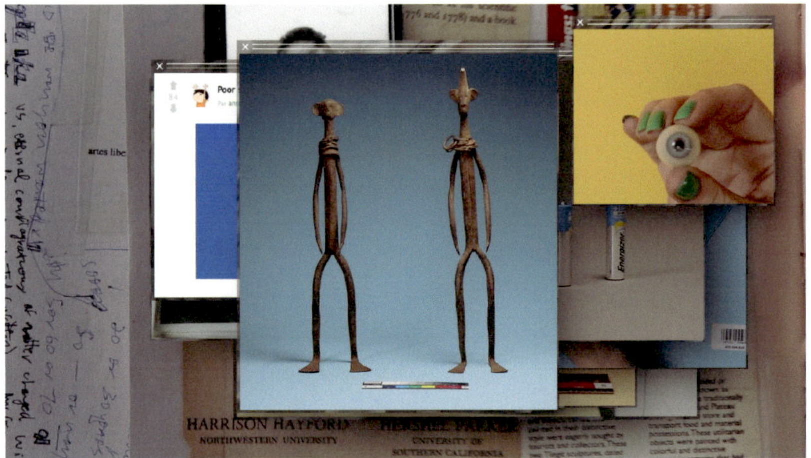

FIG 16 Camille Henrot (French; b. Paris, 1978), still image from *Grosse Fatigue*, presented at the 55th Venice Biennale, 2013

quiet study, but also as significant cultural artifacts worthy of display and representative of the networks and infrastructures through which exhibition making occurs. By featuring archival materials, *Art's Biggest Stage* also allows us to consider archival practice as a political act. More than objective record keepers, archivists have the power to shape the ways that communities and individuals' lives are made legible or obscured within the collections that we care for and describe. Largely shot at the Smithsonian Institution in Washington, DC, Camille Henrot's 2013 video *Grosse Fatigue* tackles the representation of culture and ecology within museum and archival institutions, as well as within dense networks of digital information (fig. 16). Archivists apply ordering logics that are historically situated and culturally biased, weaving layers of language and data through which the events of the past are made accessible in the present. Through the labor of archivists, students, and staff, the Clark's Venice Biennale archive makes the event accessible to scholars, artists, and others who cannot experience it in the present. My hope is that making visible the complexities of archival research and the theories, labor, and power relationships embedded in archives will open up new modes of engaging with *Art's Biggest Stage* and the Venice Biennale Ephemera Collection.

The Venice Biennale, Contemporary Art, and Aesthetics of Experience

The Venice Biennale has a long history and an international scope: debuting in 1895, it draws heavily on the model of global spectacle

SARAH HAMERMAN

embodied in nineteenth-century world's fairs (fig. 17). Today, the primary international exhibition is accompanied by independently curated national pavilions, numbering eighty-six in 2017, and a variety of collateral exhibitions dotted throughout the city of Venice; the most recent Biennale attracted over half a million visitors during its six-month run. While a printed catalogue accompanies the international exhibition and some national pavilions, much of the printed ephemera that captures the range of works exhibited is difficult to obtain without attending the Biennale in person. Recognizing the relative lack of documentation available to US-based researchers, the Clark's library launched an initiative in 2007 to comprehensively collect ephemera related to the fair. Working with bookseller Thomas Heneage, who gathers printed matter and other materials at the Biennale's professional-preview days, the Clark has amassed a vast collection ranging from press releases and posters to tote bags, USB media drives, and digital content.[1]

Unlike more recently established biennial exhibitions, the Venice Biennale has its own publicly accessible archive, the Archivio Storico delle Arti Contemporaneo (ASAC). Established in 1928 and located in Venice, ASAC consists of a research library containing over 150,000 volumes and a historical archive gathering material about the Biennale from its inception to the present. Still, academic literature on the Biennale has been slow to develop, reflecting the difficulty of accessing primary source material on the fair outside of its host city; critical literature on the subject is often by

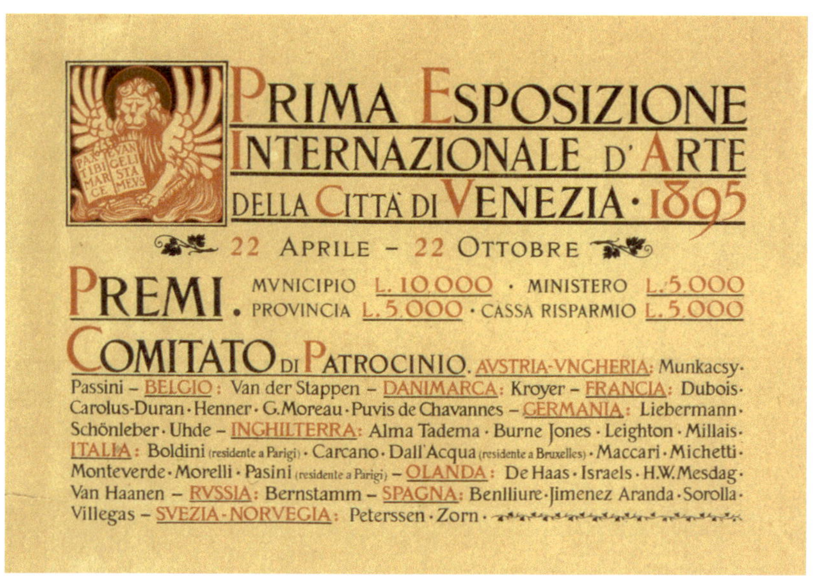

FIG 17 Exhibition announcement for the inaugural Venice Biennale, 1895

individuals directly involved with the biennial industry.[2] Much ephemeral material related to the Venice Biennale is intended for tourists, press, collectors, and other on-site visitors, and is not widely distributed elsewhere. Thus, *in situ* collection of printed matter and timely capture of born-digital material are the most thorough means by which international institutions such as the Clark are able to archive the Biennale.

Perusing the objects in the Clark's Venice Biennale archive offers a view of the ways that the art of the Biennale circulates across networks of artists and viewers, curators and galleries, funders and critics, institutions and nations. Many of these objects function simultaneously as advertisement, artist's multiple, and souvenir, giving insight into the intersection between tourism and cultural capital at play during the fair. While the individual objects in the archive preserve access to specific exhibitions, artworks, and events, the collection as a whole highlights how the discourses of the "contemporary" operate and shift throughout the Biennale's recent history. Art historian Caroline Jones cites curator Rosa Martínez, who argues that "museums are temples for the preservation of memory . . . biennials are a context for the exploration and questioning of the present."[3] While this statement asserts the relevance of the biennial format to our present context, art historian Paul O'Neill contends that it marks a shift in emphasis from art institutions to art markets. According to O'Neill, "biennials often end up promoting the concept of the contemporary, less as a rejection of the past than as a vehicle for art's cooptation into the marketplace."[4] For Jones, these conceptions of contemporaneity may take on a particular shape within the twenty-first-century cultural and political climate, but their roots are evident within the deep history of the Venice Biennale as a nineteenth-century institution. She writes: "When we look beyond claims to futurity or assertions of contemporaneity, we can begin to see the historical connections linking biennials to world's fairs, tourism, and spectacular urbanism, with implications for the efficacy and purpose of these exhibitions for the present."[5]

Over the past few decades, the Venice Biennale and similarly structured exhibitions have embraced installation art and site-specific works as dominant cultural forms (fig. 18). These ephemeral artistic strategies advance a model of art-as-experience that reshapes the Biennale's relationship to spectacle and the urban environment. For critics of art biennials, the experiential nature of immersive and site-specific installations is bound up in the tourist economy and the place-based marketing of Venice and other biennial host cities. According to O'Neill, "demands for site-specific work cause values such as authenticity, originality, and singularity to be evacuated from the work

　　　　SARAH HAMERMAN

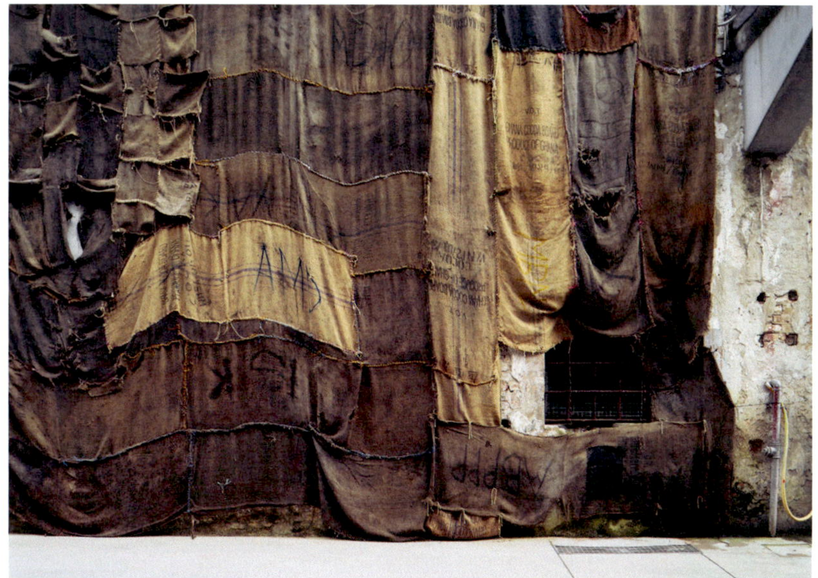

FIG 18 Ibrahim Mahama (Ghanaian; b. Tamale, 1987), installation view of *Out of Bounds*, from the main exhibition of the 56th Venice Biennale, 2015. © The artist. Photo © Ibrahim Mahama, courtesy White Cube

and transferred onto the site."[6] Such artworks often participate in an economy in which sites are overinvested with notions of authenticity and history and repackaged as tourist spectacle. Jones contends that prevalent contemporary art forms offer "experience embedded within an urban spectacle that itself is mobilized as a tourist experience."[7]

Whatever position we take on installation art and its relation to contemporaneity and the Venice Biennale as a whole, the transitory and place-based nature of these artworks presents important consequences for their preservation and documentation. Art librarians Alexander Watkins and Jane Thaler liken the documentation of biennials to the documentation of other time-based art forms. They write, "biennials are transitory and ephemeral events, and they should be considered alongside other aesthetic experiences such as performance art, intervention, social practice, and additional non-objective work."[8] Performances are often represented by photographic surrogates, which often narrow the complexity of these events to a single moment or perspective (fig. 19). According to Watkins and Thaler: "Biennials face a similar risk, as a single exhibition catalog can reduce a complex and multi-dimensional event to a single curated story. The collection of documentation and its intellectual organization in libraries and archives can help evoke the multifaceted nature of these complex events by bringing together images, video artifacts, and ephemera."[9]

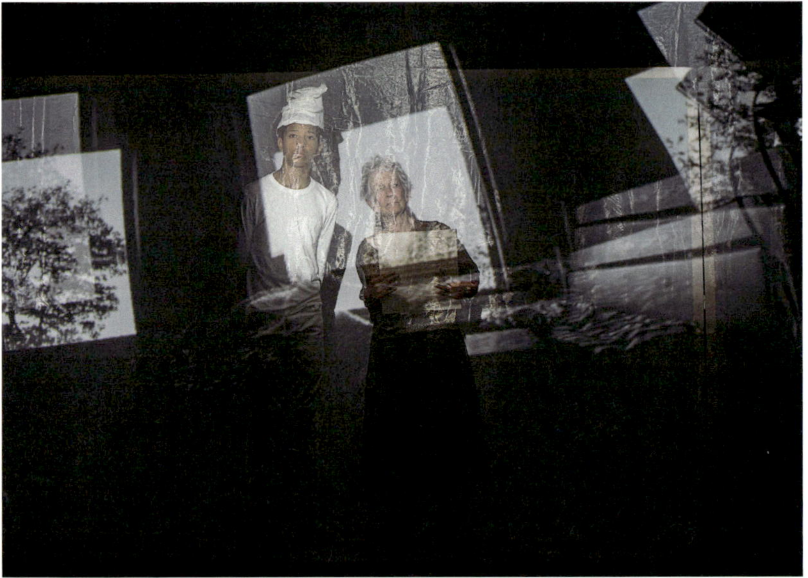

FIG 19 Joan Jonas (American; b. New York City, 1936), still image from *They Come to Us Without a Word II*, performance from the United States Pavilion of the 56th Venice Biennale, 2015

Biennials are both ephemeral events and containers of a multitude of ephemeral works, presenting archivists with additional challenges of scale and complexity. Rather than a single-authored exhibition, archivists are tasked with documenting a vast array of separately curated exhibitions that mobilize global networks of capital, institutions, and cultural producers.

Contesting the "Global" in Biennial Studies and Critical Archival Practice

Comprehensively collecting ephemera related to the Venice Biennale and making it available for public study does a great deal to democratize engagement with the Biennale's contemporary histories. Still, the process of archiving should not be understood as neutral or mechanical record keeping, nor can any archive ever present a complete picture of its domain. Like the biennial exhibition format, modern library and archival science traces its roots to the nineteenth century, founded on aspirations of universality and neutrality that were rooted in colonial projects of classification and control. In *The Imperial Archive,* Thomas Richards traces archival science back to Victorian England, where the systematic organization of information serviced the exercise of power across an empire with global reach.[10] Likewise, the first of

                                        SARAH HAMERMAN

the industrial World's Fairs took place at London's Crystal Palace in 1851, showcasing national identity and evolving technology on a global stage. In the case of both the Biennale and archival science, exclusions and biases are concealed by such claims to completeness. In recent years, both the Venice Biennale and the field of archival science have embraced postcolonial and deconstructionist perspectives that have questioned their Eurocentric intellectual foundations. Archiving provides a context through which we can trace the Venice Biennale's relationship to evolving considerations of the global. At the same time, we must recognize archiving itself as a situated act.

The inaugural Venice Biennale took place just one year before the 1896 launch of the modern Olympic Games, and, like the Olympics, the Biennale's national pavilion system secures and projects national identities in the context of an international spectacle. As Caroline Jones writes, "biennials and world's fairs conduct politics by other means."[11] The pavilion system has expanded well beyond its Eurocentric foundations in recent years, but critics, artists, and curators continue to debate the kinds of national representations encouraged by the biennial system. According to Jones, "National pavilions . . . made manifest the formulae by which artists would become 'representative,' demanding that artists or objects transmit national or ethnic meaning while insisting that they use international styles to do so."[12] Critic Jan Verwoert laments the rise of a contemporary "biennial art" that trivializes cultural exchange rather than deepening it by circulating tokenistic representations of cultural diversity.[13] Still, the biennial has included some meaningful attempts to critique its colonial and nationalist legacies, such as Okwui Enwezor's 2015 *All the World's Futures* exhibition (fig. 20).

Critical archival theory articulates how archival practices of collection and description are acts of power. This discourse offers important tools for considering the Biennale and its archive's role in globalization, colonialism, and our assessment of the contemporary. Recent artistic and curatorial practice has often referred to "the archive" as a kind of metaphorical abstraction for the accumulation of historical records. Critical archival theory clarifies this discourse by considering specific archives as contested spaces, constantly reshaped by the decisions archivists make in relation to the subjects and users of their records. According to Joan M. Schwartz and Terry Cook, "archives have the power to privilege and to marginalize. They can be a tool of hegemony; they can be a tool of resistance. They both reflect and constitute power relations."[14] This conception of archives as contested sites has been more broadly accepted in the field in recent decades, marking

ALL THE WORLD'S FUTURES

Biennale Arte
09.05 – 22.11.2015

Venezia
Giardini – Arsenale
Orario / hours 10-18

Chiuso il lunedì
Closed on Mondays
www.labiennale.org

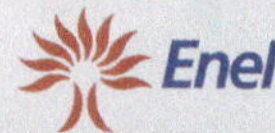

swatch

FIG 20 Brochure from *All the World's Futures*, main exhibition of the 56th Venice Biennale, 2015. 8¼ × 6¼ in. (21 × 16 cm). Clark Art Institute Library, Venice Biennale Ephemera Collection

a substantial shift from prior conceptions of archival professionals as objective and neutral.

Michelle Caswell identifies the concepts of the "record," provenance, and value as three key tenets of archival studies that have been given more nuanced and justice-driven meanings by critical archival theorists. Records are the core unit of archival collections, and they are traditionally understood as evidence of past action. Whereas the evidentiary model sees records as relatively fixed, pluralist and deconstructionist archival theorists such as Eric Ketelaar see "records as dynamic objects in motion, continually shifting with each new use and contextualization."[15] Recognizing the importance of community within oral traditions, Shannon Faulkhead, an archivist of Koori descent focused on Australian Indigenous archives, describes the record as "a springboard for memory."[16] Rather than applying external classification schema, archival science arranges records by their *provenance*, "insist[ing] on the importance of the context of the record, even over and above its content."[17] Archival provenance has historically privileged the "original order" defined by the records' creator, but has broadened to include the records' subjects as well as the archivists and users who interpret them. Centering the subjects of records, rather than only their creators, is a primary means by which archivists can redress the violence of colonial record-keeping. For postcolonial archivists, "provenance becomes a tool for community inclusion, rather than one of limitation. . . ."[18] Finally, the notion of archival *value* is exercised primarily through the process of appraisal and selection, when archivists decide which records are to be kept as enduring representation of past events. The act of appraisal is rooted in institutional context and is one of the major ways in which archivists' political, cultural, and historical biases can shape collective memory. According to Caswell, "this assignation of value is perhaps the greatest expression of archival power and expertise, through which archivists act as gatekeepers to the past."[19]

While evolving considerations of provenance and the record offer tools to assess the materials we encounter *in* an archive, the notion of archival value points to the critical question of an archive's gaps and absences. Contending with what an archive *excludes* is a vital practice not only for the archivists who maintain collections, but also for the communities, academics, artists, and students who engage with them. According to artist Mariam Ghani: "The attraction of archives will always be as much about what they lack as what they contain. Those gaps and holes, all the things left unfinished, are often the possibilities: the cracks where your own imaginings of the archive can creep in, and the sites where earlier resistance to the dominant narrative of the archive has already taken root."[20] Ghani's statement is beautifully evoked by Joana Hadjithomas and Khalil Joriege's artists' book, *Latent Images: Diary of a Photographer*, presented as a series of daily readings at the 2015 Venice Biennale. The project focuses on the work of Lebanese postcard photographer Abdullah Farah, who shot, but never developed, hundreds of rolls of film during the Lebanese civil war. Farah meticulously documented each undeveloped photograph in his diary with a written description. In its tension between absence and record, *Latent Images* reveals how archival silences can be sites not only of historical meaning, but also, potentially, of trauma (fig. 21).

Critical archival practice can be a powerful tool for amplifying those voices that have been marginalized. Beyond expanding the archive, these practices can also highlight archival gaps as sites of violence and trauma that are constitutive of archival and historical "truth." Archives also operate within a continuum of institutional contexts, from the public and academic to closed corporate and governmental archives. Thus, archival exclusion may be a question of access as much as one of preservation.

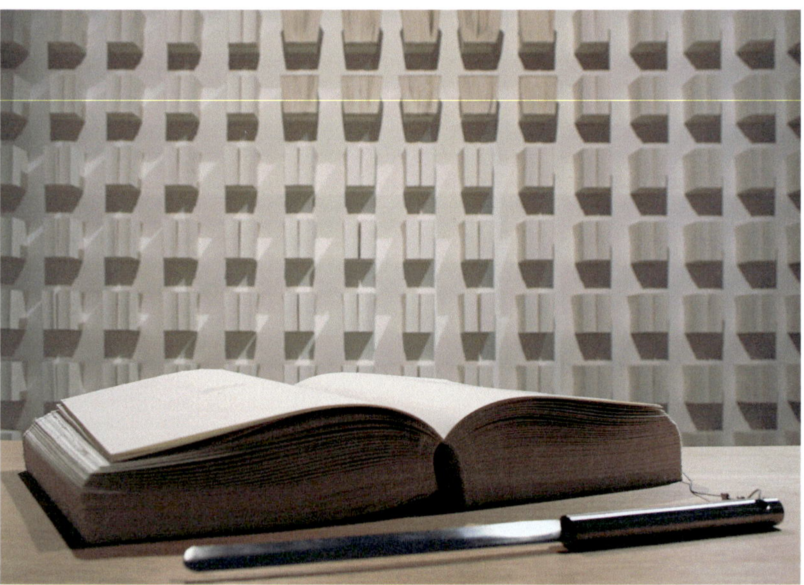

FIG 21 Joana Hadjithomas (Lebanese; b. Beirut, 1969) and Khalil Joriege (Lebanese; b. Beirut, 1969), installation view of *Latent Images: Diary of a Photographer*, *177 Days of Performance*, presented at the 56th Venice Biennale, 2015

SARAH HAMERMAN

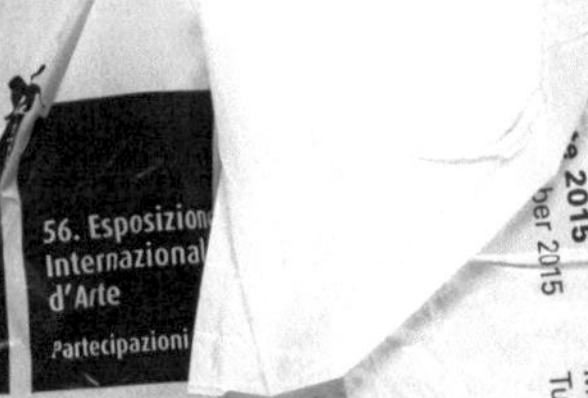

FIG 22 Simon Denny (New Zealand; b. Auckland, 1982), plastic bag from *Secret Power*, New Zealand Pavilion of the 56th Venice Biennale, 2015. 23 ¼ × 11 ¾ in. (59 × 30 cm). Clark Art Institute Library, Venice Biennale Ephemera Collection

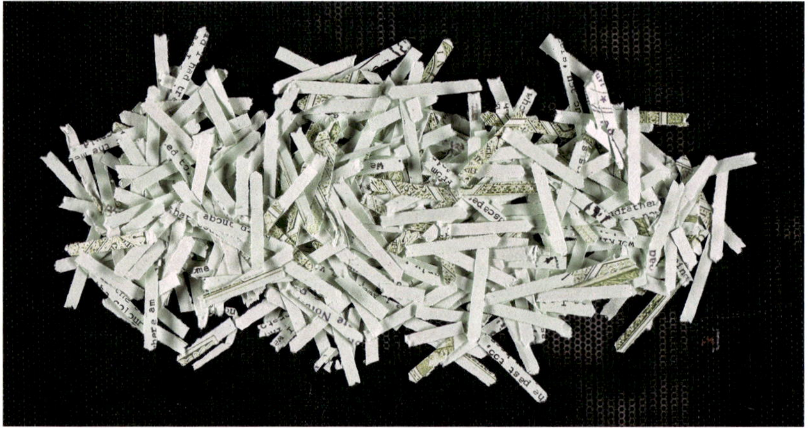

FIG 23 Shilpa Gupta (Indian; b. Mumbai, 1976), pieces of paper from *Witness Is Denial,* from *My East Is Your West*, collateral event of the 56th Venice Biennale, 2015. Clark Art Institute Library, Venice Biennale Ephemera Collection

Artistic and curatorial strategies, with their emphasis on the visual, spatial, and dialogical, perhaps offer more adept means than strict academic research for addressing archival absence and cultural visibility. Simon Denny's 2015 Venice Biennale exhibition *Secret Power*, in the New Zealand pavilion, explored the NSA's graphic identity and iconography in the wake of revelations about mass citizen surveillance by whistleblower Edward Snowden (fig. 22). Highlighting how governmental secrecy makes possible the mass collection of individuals' telecommunications metadata, Denny highlights the asymmetries of power and information at the heart of contemporary governance.[21] Indian artist Shilpa Gupta's *Witness Is Denial*, presented as part of a collateral event at the 2015 Biennale, evokes issues of borders, cultural conflict, and (in)visibility through an installation of envelopes containing shredded paper fragments (fig. 23).[22]

As we engage with archival collections, we encounter not only paper, objects, and data, but also sites of sociality where voices from the past, present, and future convene. As Ghani writes: "Each archive has its archivists and administrators, janitors and historians, redactors and readers, and others who at various times perform the archive for its public. Each performance refracts the archive through the performer's interpretation, and each is then reflected in the archive, as the interpretation becomes another record, or another path through the records that can be retraced."[23]

While many of these performances, or kinds of labor, often occur in the background, they inevitably shape the meanings that we can draw from and rewrite around archival collections. The more that we consider archival traces as embodied traces, reflective of affective value

SARAH HAMERMAN

as much as institutional value, the deeper the meanings we are able to draw from archives. As we consider questions of globalism, spectacle, and contemporaneity around *Art's Biggest Stage* and the Venice Biennale since 2007, we might approach the exhibition as a single "performance" of the archive, in Ghani's words. While all archives are "living" to some degree, the Clark's Venice Biennale archive is especially so, allowing us to revisit and reassess the multiple stories contained within it as the archive grows with each new iteration of the event.

1 Susan Roeper, "Bringing the Biennale Home: Contemporary Collecting in the Clark Library," *Journal of the Clark* 18 (2017), 31.

2 Gustavo Grandal Montero, "Biennialization? What Biennialization? Documentation of Biennials and Other Recurrent Exhibitions," *Art Libraries Journal* 37/1 (2011): 16.

3 Caroline Jones, "Biennial Culture: A Longer History," in *The Biennial Reader,* ed. Elena Filipovic, Marieke van Hal, Solveig Øvstebø (Berlin: Hatje Cantz, 2010), 72.

4 Paul O'Neill, *The Culture of Curating and the Curating of Culture(s)* (Cambridge: MIT Press, 2012), 54.

5 Jones, "Biennial Culture," 68.

6 O'Neill, *The Culture of Curating*, 74.

7 Jones, "Biennial Culture," 82.

8 Alexander Watkins and Jane Thaler, "Collecting, Organizing and Teaching the Ephemera of Art Biennials," *Art Documentation* 37, no. 1 (Spring 2018): 74.

9 Ibid., 75.

10 Okwui Enwezor, *Archive Fever: Uses of the Document in Contemporary Art* (New York: International Center of Photography, 2008), 18; see also Thomas Richards, *The Imperial Archive: Knowledge and the Fantasy of Empire* (London: Verso, 1993).

11 Jones, "Biennial Culture," 77.

12 Ibid., 82.

13 Jan Verwoert, "The Curious Case of Biennial Art," in *The Biennial Reader,* 87.

14 Joan M. Schwartz and Terry Cook, "Archives, Records, and Power: The Making of Modern Memory," in *Archival Science*, no. 2 (2002): 13.

15 Michelle Caswell, "'The Archive' is not an Archives: Acknowledging the Contributions of Archival Studies," in *Reconstruction: Studies in Contemporary Culture* 16, no. 1 (2016); see also Eric Ketelaar, "Tacit Narratives: The Meaning of Archives," in *Archival Science* 1, no. 2 (2001): 138.

16 Caswell, "'The Archive' is not an Archives."

17–19 Ibid.

20 Mariam Ghani, "What We Left Unfinished: The Artist and the Archive," in *Dissonant Archives: Contemporary Visual Culture and Contested Narrative in the Middle East,* ed. Anthony Downey (London: I.B. Tauris, 2015), 62.

21 "Simon Denny 'Secret Power' at the New Zealand Pavilion Venice," in *Mousse Magazine* (2015), http://moussemagazine.it/simon-denny-new-zealand-venice/.

22 "My East is Your West," blog post, http://masterpiecesmnba.blogspot.com/2015/07/my-east-is-your-west.html.

23 Ghani, "What We Left Unfinished," 45.

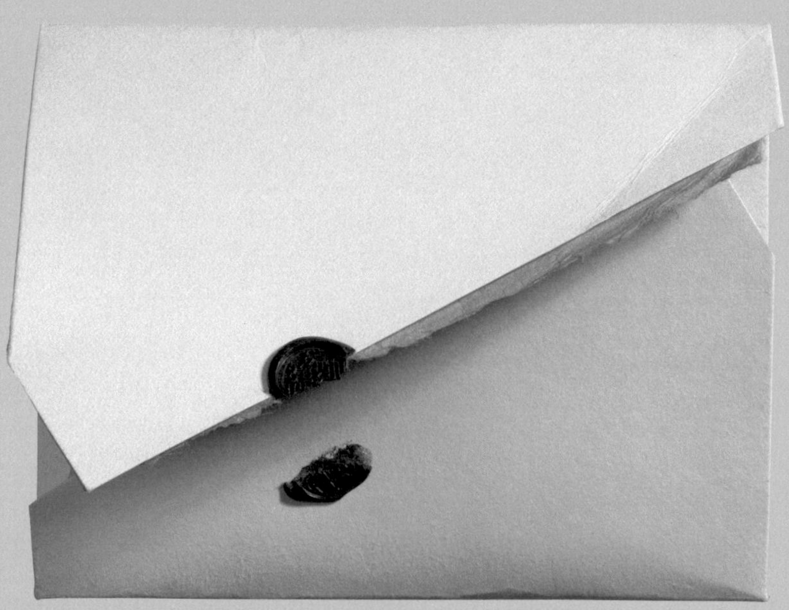

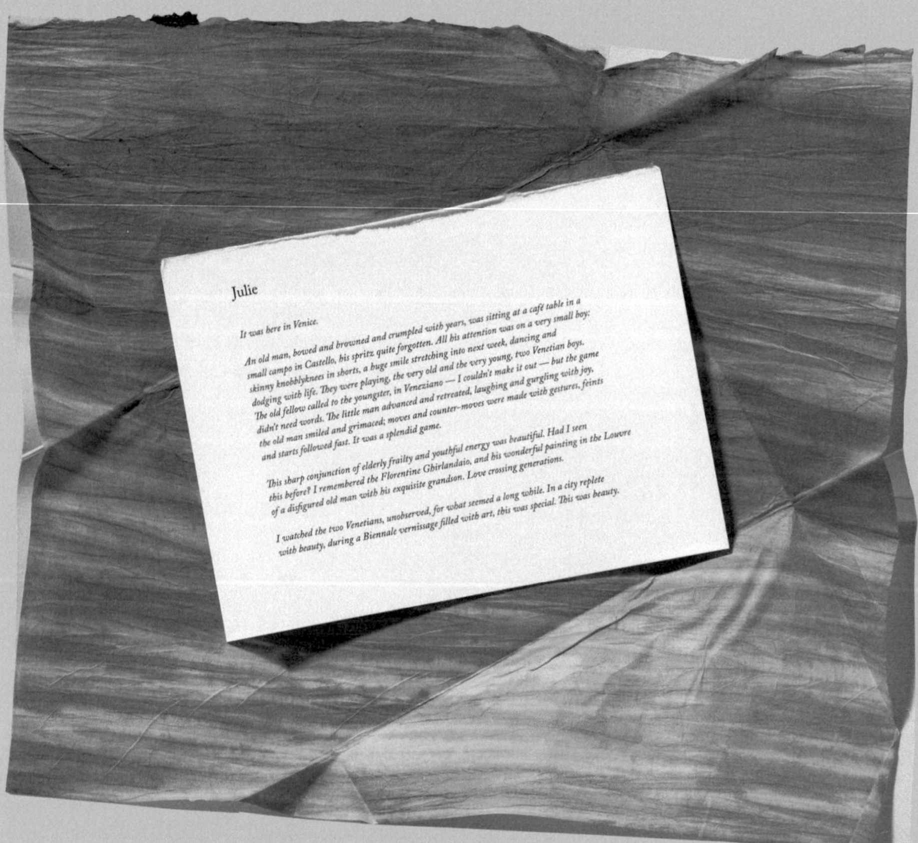

Julie

It was here in Venice.

An old man, bowed and browned and crumpled with years, was sitting at a café table in a small campo in Castello, his spritz quite forgotten. All his attention was on a very small boy: skinny knobblyknees in shorts, a huge smile stretching into next week, dancing and dodging with life. They were playing, the very old and the very young, two Venetian boys. The old fellow called to the youngster, in Veneziano — I couldn't make it out — but the game didn't need words. The little man advanced and retreated, laughing and gurgling with joy; the old man smiled and grimaced; moves and counter-moves were made with gestures, feints and starts followed fast. It was a splendid game.

This sharp conjunction of elderly frailty and youthful energy was beautiful. Had I seen this before? I remembered the Florentine Ghirlandaio, and his wonderful painting in the Louvre of a disfigured old man with his exquisite grandson. Love crossing generations.

I watched the two Venetians, unobserved, for what seemed a long while. In a city replete with beauty, during a Biennale vernissage filled with art, this was special. This was beauty.

Julie

It was here in Venice.

An old man, bowed and browned and crumpled with years, was sitting at a café table in a small campo in Castello, his spritz quite forgotten. All his attention was on a very small boy: skinny knobblyknees in shorts, a huge smile stretching into next week, dancing and dodging with life. They were playing, the very old and the very young, two Venetian boys. The old fellow called to the youngster, in Veneziano — I couldn't make it out — but the game didn't need words. The little man advanced and retreated, laughing and gurgling with joy, the old man smiled and grimaced; moves and counter-moves were made with gestures, feints and starts followed fast. It was a splendid game.

This sharp conjunction of elderly frailty and youthful energy was beautiful. Had I seen this before? I remembered the Florentine Ghirlandaio, and his wonderful painting in the Louvre of a disfigured old man with his exquisite grandson. Love crossing generations.

I watched the two Venetians, unobserved, for what seemed a long while. In a city replete with beauty, during a Biennale vernissage filled with art, this was special. This was beauty.

CAT 80

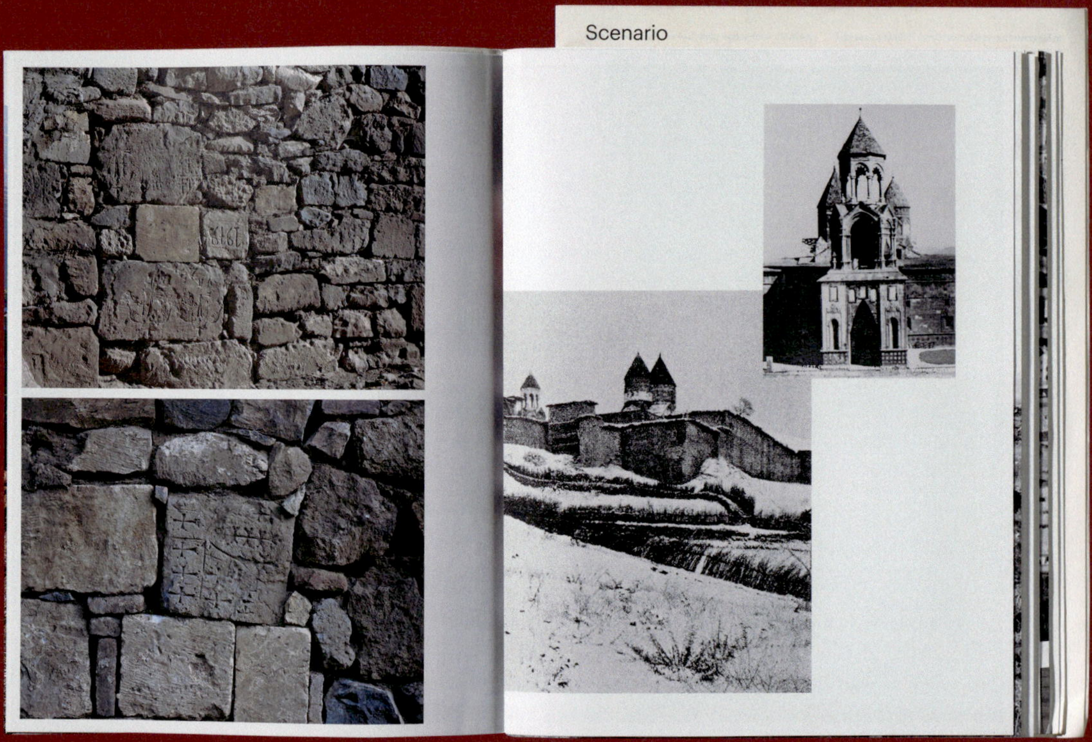
Scenario

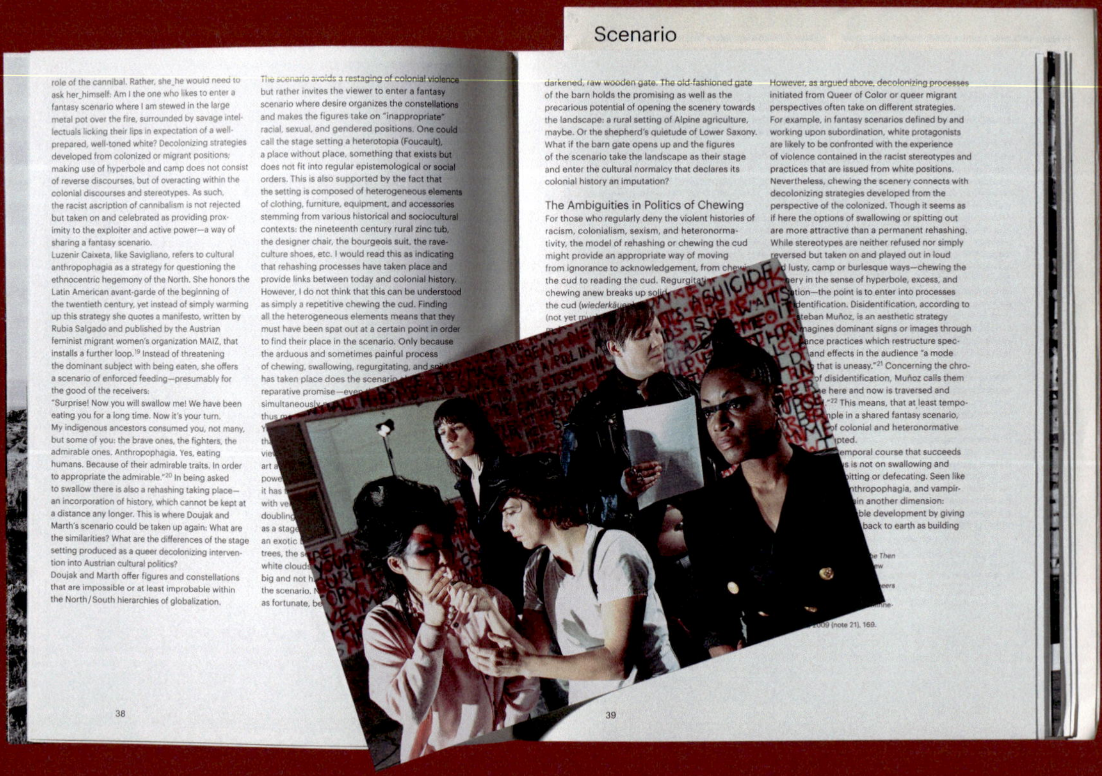
Scenario
role of the cannibal. Rather, she_he would need to ask her_himself: Am I the one who likes to enter a fantasy scenario where I am stewed in the large metal pot over the fire, surrounded by savage intellectuals licking their lips in expectation of a well-prepared, well-toned white? Decolonizing strategies developed from colonized or migrant positions; making use of hyperbole and camp does not consist of reverse discourses, but of overacting within the colonial discourses and stereotypes. As such, the racist ascription of cannibalism is not rejected but taken on and celebrated as providing proximity to the exploiter and active power—a way of sharing a fantasy scenario.
Luzenir Caixeta, like Savigliano, refers to cultural anthropophagia as a strategy for questioning the ethnocentric hegemony of the North. She honors the Latin American avant-garde of the beginning of the twentieth century, yet instead of simply warming up this strategy she quotes a manifesto, written by Rubia Salgado and published by the Austrian feminist migrant women's organization MAIZ, that installs a further loop.19 Instead of threatening the dominant subject with being eaten, she offers a scenario of enforced feeding—presumably for the good of the receivers:
"Surprise! Now you will swallow me! We have been eating you for a long time. Now it's your turn. My indigenous ancestors consumed you, not many, but some of you: the brave ones, the fighters, the admirable ones. Anthropophagia. Yes, eating humans. Because of their admirable traits. In order to appropriate the admirable."20 In being asked to swallow there is also a rehashing taking place—an incorporation of history, which cannot be kept at a distance any longer. This is where Doujak and Marth's scenario could be taken up again: What are the similarities? What are the differences of the stage setting produced as a queer decolonizing intervention into Austrian cultural politics?
Doujak and Marth offer figures and constellations that are impossible or at least improbable within the North/South hierarchies of globalization.
The scenario avoids a restaging of colonial violence but rather invites the viewer to enter a fantasy scenario where desire organizes the constellations and makes the figures take on "inappropriate" racial, sexual, and gendered positions. One could call the stage setting a heterotopia (Foucault), a place without place, something that exists but does not fit into regular epistemological or social orders. This is also supported by the fact that the setting is composed of heterogeneous elements of clothing, furniture, equipment, and accessories stemming from various historical and sociocultural contexts: the nineteenth century rural zinc tub, the designer chair, the bourgeois suit, the rave-culture shoes, etc. I would read this as indicating that rehashing processes have taken place and provide links between today and colonial history. However, I do not think that this can be understood as simply a repetitive chewing the cud. Finding all the heterogeneous elements means that they must have been spat out at a certain point in order to find their place in the scenario. Only because the arduous and sometimes painful process of chewing, swallowing, regurgitating, and
has taken place does the scenario
reparative promise—even
simultaneously
darkened, raw wooden gate. The old-fashioned gate of the barn holds the promising as well as the precarious potential of opening the scenery towards the landscape: a rural setting of Alpine agriculture, maybe. Or the shepherd's quietude of Lower Saxony. What if the barn gate opens up and the figures of the scenario take the landscape as their stage and enter the cultural normalcy that declares its colonial history an imputation?
The Ambiguities in Politics of Chewing
For those who regularly deny the violent histories of racism, colonialism, sexism, and heteronormativity, the model of rehashing or chewing the cud might provide an appropriate way of moving from ignorance to acknowledgement, from
the cud to reading the cud. Regurgitat
chewing anew breaks up soli
the cud (wiederkäu
However, as argued above, decolonizing processes initiated from Queer of Color or queer migrant perspectives often take on different strategies. For example, in fantasy scenarios defined by and working upon subordination, white protagonists are likely to be confronted with the experience of violence contained in the racist stereotypes and practices that are issued from white positions. Nevertheless, chewing the scenery connects with decolonizing strategies developed from the perspective of the colonized. Though it seems as if here the options of swallowing or spitting out are more attractive than a permanent rehashing. While stereotypes are neither refused nor simply reversed but taken on and played out in loud
lusty, camp or burlesque ways—chewing the
ery in the sense of hyperbole, excess, and
tion—the point is to enter into processes
dentification. Disidentification, according to
steban Muñoz, is an aesthetic strategy
magines dominant signs or images through
ance practices which restructure spec-
and effects in the audience "a mode
that is uneasy."21 Concerning the chro-
of disidentification, Muñoz calls them
e here and now is traversed and
"22 This means, that at least tempo-
ple in a shared fantasy scenario,
of colonial and heteronormative
pted.
emporal course that succeeds
is not on swallowing and
pitting or defecating. Seen like
nthropophagia, and vampir-
in another dimension:
ble development by giving
back to earth as building
SUICIDE
38
39

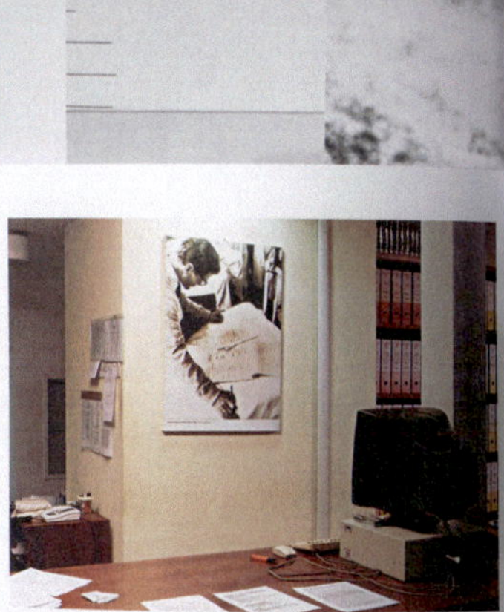

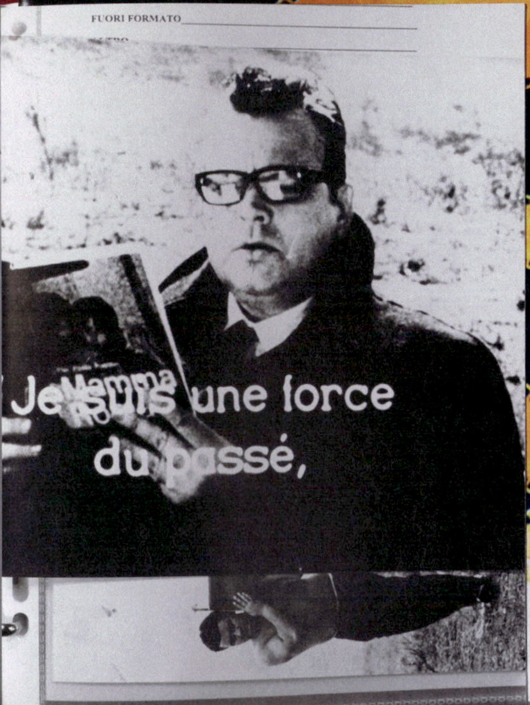

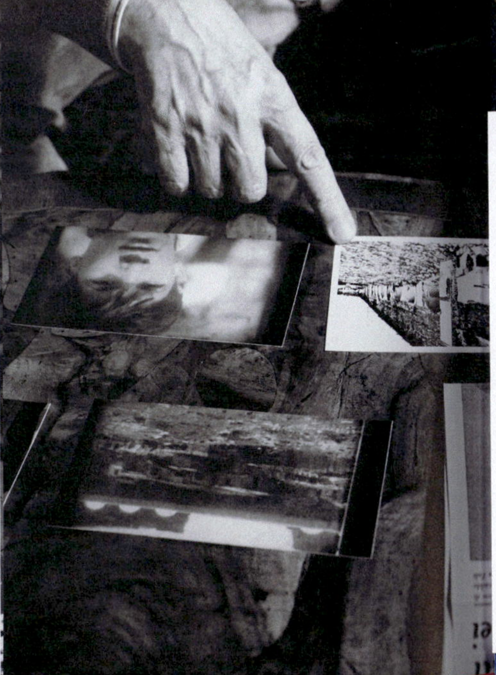

zione, o meglio ancora, per usare quel termine che pone in crisi lo strutturalismo (soprattutto se inteso convenzionalmente, come da certi gruppi italiani), un termine del Murdock, un vero e proprio « processo ». Ma un processo particolare, non trattandosi di un'evoluzione, di un passaggio da uno stadio A a uno stadio B: ma di un puro e semplice « dinamismo », di una « tensione », che si muove, senza partire e senza arrivare, da una struttura stilistica, quella della narrativa, a un'altra struttura stilistica, quella del cinema, e, più profondamente, da un sistema linguistico a un altro.

La « struttura » dinamica ma senza funzionalità, e fuori dalle leggi dell'evoluzione, dello sceno-testo, si presta perfettamente come oggetto per uno scontro tra il concetto ormai tradizionale di « struttura » e quello critico di « processo ». Murdock e Vogt si troverebbero davanti a un « processo che non procede », a una struttura che fa del processo la propria caratteristica strutturale; Lévi-Strauss si troverebbe davanti non ai valori di una « filosofia ingenua », che determinano i processi « direzionali », ma davanti a una vera e propria volontà di movimento, la volontà dell'autore che designando i significati di una struttura linguistica come i segni tipici di quella struttura, nel tempo stesso designa i significati di un'altra struttura. Tale volontà è precisa: è un dato di fatto, che l'osservatore può osservare dall'esterno, di cui è egli stesso testimone. Non è una volontà ipotizzata e ingenuamente provata. La sincronia del sistema degli sceno-testi pone come elemento fondamentale la diacronia. Ossia, ripeto, il processo. *Abbiamo così nel laboratorio una struttura morfologicamente in movimento.*

Che un individuo, in quanto autore, reagisca al sistema costruendone un altro, mi sembra semplice e naturale; così come gli uomini, in quanto autori di storia, reagiscono alla struttura sociale costruendone un'altra, attraverso la rivoluzione, ossia alla volontà di trasformare la struttura. Non intendo quindi parlare, secondo la critica sociologica americana, di valori e volizioni « naturali » e ontologici: ma parlo di « volontà rivoluzionaria » sia nell'autore in quanto creatore di un sistema stilistico individuale che contraddice il sistema grammaticale e letterario-gergale vigente, sia negli uomini in quanto sovvertitori di sistemi politici.

Nel caso di un autore di sceno-testi, e, più ancora, di film, siamo davanti a un fatto curioso: la presenza di un sistema stilistico là dove non è ancora definito un sistema linguistico, e dove la struttura non è cosciente e descritta scientificamente. Un regista, met-

195

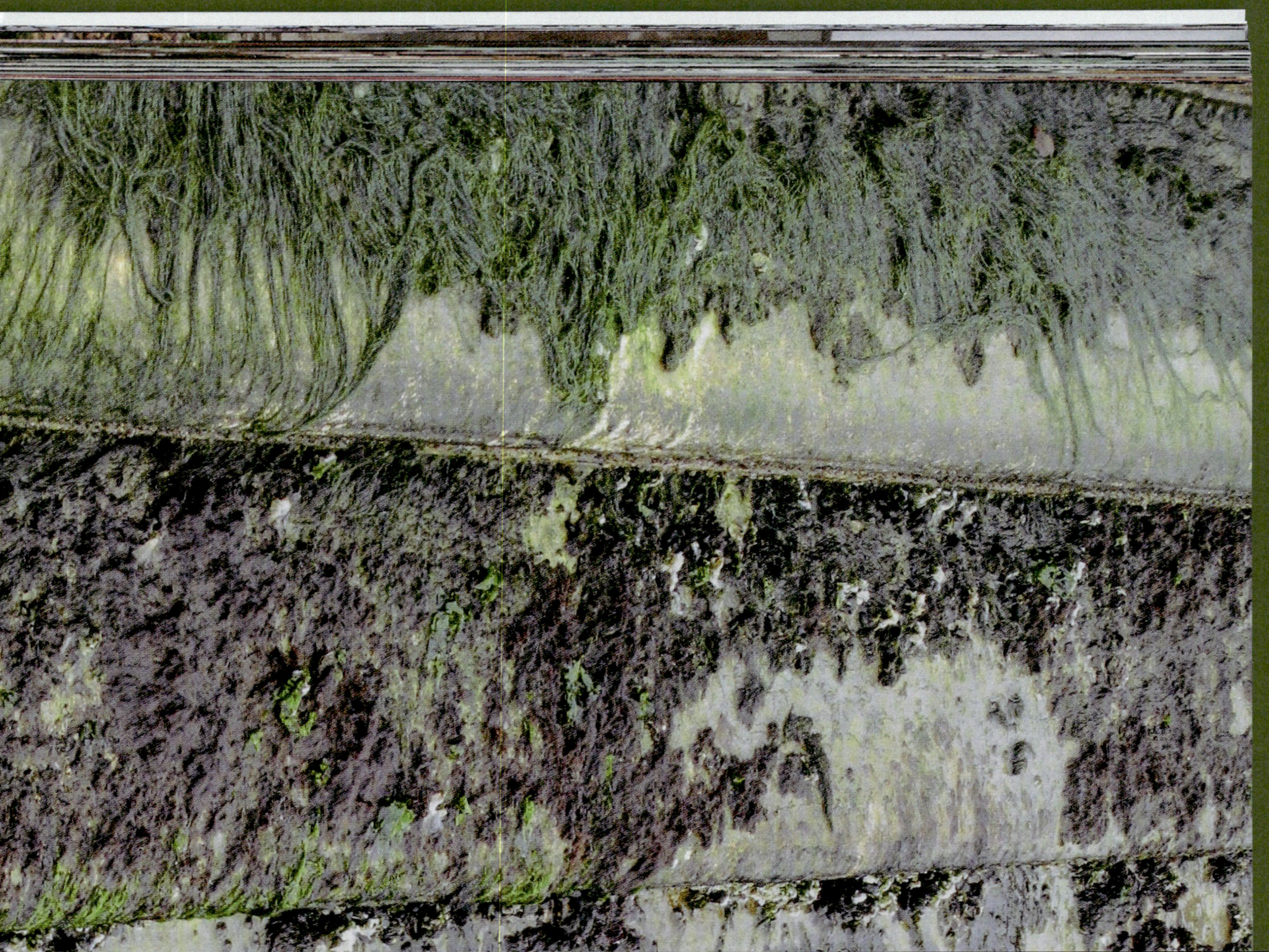

حول اعمال خمسة فنانين تشكيليين مكرمين

نجاة مكي مرحلة متقدمة في مسار الحركة التشكيلية في الامارات
وعبدالرحيم سالم اسير الواقعية المباشرة رغم محاولته الانفلات منها
الشرح اضعف ملصقات محمد مندي وعبيد سرور يكرر نفسه

د. محمود أمهز

محمد القصاب

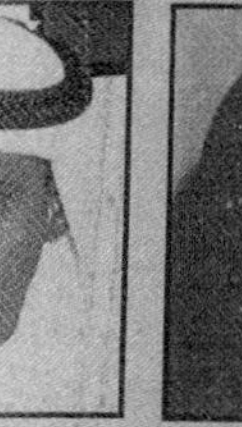

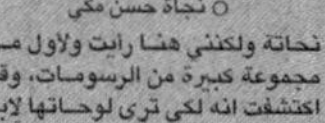
○ نجاة حسن مكي

اعتدنا، وربما اعتاد معظم الفنانين التشكيليين على ان تقام المعارض العامة وتتابع اعلامياً ويرافقها ما يرافقها من ندوات ومحاضرات ويزورها الزائرون، ثم يعود كل من حيث اتى دون ان يسمع الفنان وجهة نظر واحدة في اعماله، وان حدث وقيل رأي فهو يقال في حدود ضيقة للغاية او بين زميلين.

يهذا التباين الكبير بين اعماله، وبحيث يمكننا ان نربط بين هذه الاعمال بما تعكسه من معالم شخصية واضحة ومحددة.

اما عن اهم ما استوقفه في تجربة فناني الامارات فيقول:

لم اكن اتوقع ان ارى ما رايت في الامارات، وما اثار اهتمامي وانتباهي هو مايلفته هذه الحركة الفنية في مجملها رغم كل الملاحظات النقدية التي اثرنا اليها فاستوقفتني بعض الاعمال، مثل اعمال نجاة حسن، وعبدالرحيم سالم، وعبداللطيف الصمودي، وبخاصة اعمال حسن شريف التي تشكل رغم ارتباطها بتجارب مماثلة حصلت في الغرب تشكل ظاهرة خاصة ومميزة بالنسبة للامارات وللمنطقة العربية بوجه عام، فاختيار هذا النمط الفني المفاهيمي الرافض للفن بشكل بحد ذاته محاولة شجاعة وجريئة، فضلا عن انها ذات مميزات خاصة حتى اذا ما قورنت بمثيلاتها الغربية.

○ محمد مندي

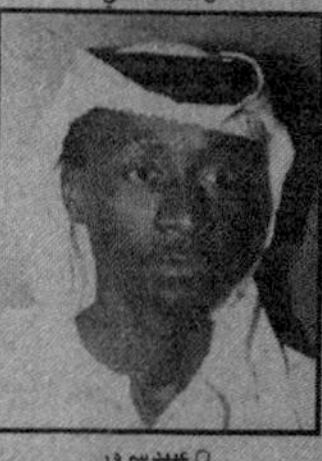

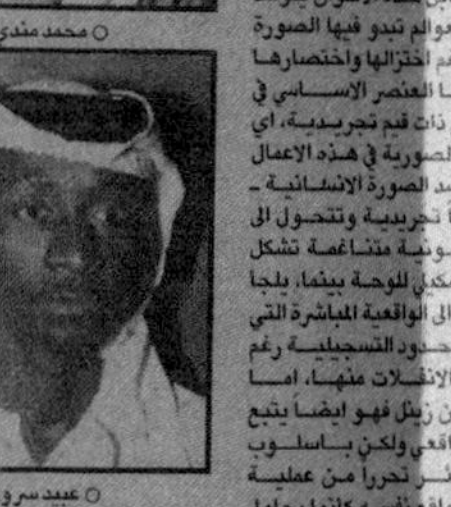
○ عبيد سرور

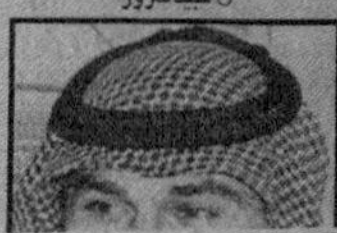

تحقيق
نجــوم الغــانم

حسن الى المساحات اللونية البارزة بحيث ان تقابل هذه الالوان بولد انطباعات بعوالم تبدو فيها الصورة الانسانية رغم اختزالها واختصارها وتبسيطها العنصر الاساسي في اللوحة وهي ذات فعل تجريبية، اي ان الاشكال الصورية في هذه الاعمال الفنية ـ بقصد الصورة الانسانية ـ تكتسب قيما تجريبية وتتحول الى مساحات لونية متناغمة تشكل الفضاء التشكيلي للوحة بينما يلجا عبيد سرور الى الواقعية المباشرة التي تبقى ضمن حدود التسجيلية رغم محاولته الانفلات منها، اما عبدالرحمن زينل فهو ايضا يتبع النهج الواقعي ولكن بـاسلوب مختلف واكبر تحررا من عملية المحاكاة للواقع نفسه كانما يحاول ان يبتعد عن هذا الواقع الذي يحاكيه باضفاء طابع الغرابة على لوحاته وذلك باستخدام ساحات لونية مونوكرومية اي ذات لون واحد فيها شيء من السوريالية.

بالنسبة الى محمد مندي فان اعماله

في المعرض الاخير الذي نظمته دائرة الثقافة والاعلام بالشارقة بالتعاون مع جمعية الامارات للفنون التشكيلية والـذي تم الاحتفال فيه بمرور عشر سنوات على تأسيس الجمعية كان اللقاء كبيرا لهذا العام بين الفنانين بسبب كثرة عدد المشاركين اولا، واتساع حجم المعرض ثانيا، حتى ان زيارة واحدة لم تكن للاطلاع على جميع اللوحات والاتجاهات، الامر الذي نظر اليه البعض على انه نوع من الخديعة، لجات اليها دائرة الثقافة والاعلام عندما جمعت بين ثلاثة معارض تقريبا في معرض واحد. الا ان هذا من وجهة نظر اخرى اعتبر «ورطة» جميلة انه جمع بين اسرة ماكانت ستجتمع لـو لم يقم بقم المعرض، وكل عام كان هناك مايشبه المهرجان الصغر الذي اتاح للكثيرين ان يلتقوا ويتبادلوا التحيات والاسئلة وان يشاهدوا جديدا كل واحد منهم ويستعيدوا بعض الذكريات، وفي هذا الملتقى طرحت فكرة ان يبدي بعضهم فتوجس البعض واعتبر من اعتز وكانت هذه الاسماء القليلة التي وافقت على ان نقـول رأيها في

نحاتة ولكنني هنا رايت ولاول مرة مجموعة كبيرة من الرسومات، وقد اكتشفت انه لكي ترى لوحاتها لابد وان تستمع لها لانها تخفي افكارا غير ظاهرة من خلال الخطوط المباشرة.

ويضيف:

رأيت ان الالوان الفسفورية التي تستخدمها هذه الفنانة واحدة من الاشياء التي تميـز اعمالها، انها صارخة وذات تأثير قوي، وطالما انها تخدم افكارها فهذا شيء جيد ولكن بودي لو كان الهدف من اللون واضحـا في اللوحة كما هـو حال الموضوع.

وعن الفنانين الاخرين يقول:

لا اعرف اعمال عبدالرحمن زينل لانه غير موجود الا في مناسبات قليلة، ربما كان السبب يرجع الى ظروف عمله، وربما لشخص خاصة بطبيعته!!

اما عبدالرحيم سالم فلا افهمه رغم ان عمله النحتي يستوقفني واحيانا اكثر من اللوحة، معرفتي بمحمد مندي انه خطاط، لكنني لاحظت انه عندما يحاول ان يزاوج بين الخط والرسم فان الرسم يضعف لوحته.

احترم انتاج عبيد سرور لأني اعتقد انه فنان مقتنع بالشكل الذي يجب ان يتخذه اسلوبا لـه، فهو ملتزم وفنا وقت مبكر يتناول كل ماهـو تراثي واظنه مازال يتناول انه بحاجة لرسم المزيد في هذا الموضوع وهـذا في رأيي

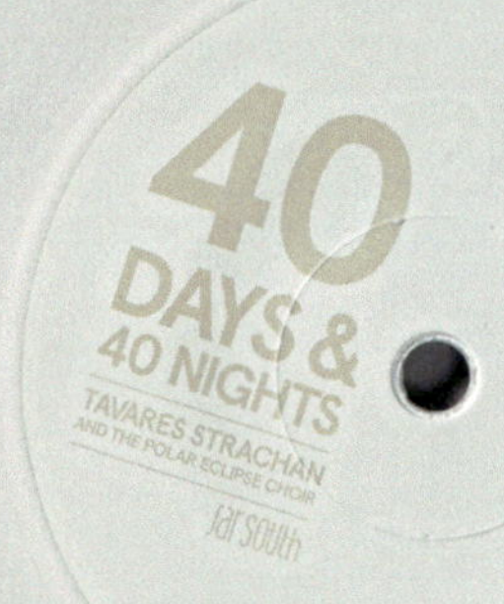

40
DAYS &
40 NIGHTS
TAVARES STRACHAN
AND THE POLAR ECLIPSE CHOIR
far south

40
DAYS &
40 NIGHTS
TAVARES STRACHAN
AND THE POLAR ECLIPSE CHOIR
far south

THE SINGERS

Je'van Lee McCoy
Javier Leanardo Forbes Jr
Sion Stephan Walkine
Perrell Emilio R M A Cooper
Ashton Jamaal Kemp
Davonte Marvin Brown
AndreTheron Rolle
Zurial Earl Carey
Koen Theodore Z Bodie
Jaden Emerick G Martinborough
Theron Caleb S Murray
Cranston O'neil Russell Jr
Percival Austyn Taylor
Gregory Duvall McKay Jr
Ivan Dae Neymour
Pariss Elizabeth Mason
Cajah Antonia Jalae Burrows
Vanessa Anari N Sherman
Merisha Kayshante Butler
Krystal Cleann Smith
Taylor Alexa Cartwright
Tyler Ashleigh Cartwright
Hannah Shakinah Duncombe
Aaliyah Alisha Goodman
Taliyah Ashanti Bain
Shanice Anastacia Farrington
Kendia Malissa Sears
Jehmeilia Tiarra Smith
Lanique Krysell A Rolle
Brazille An'tonya R Marshall
Jamie Aaliyah Emmanuel
Hadasah Mariah L Lockhart
Beyonce Shadiamond S Delancy
Asia Elizabeth Hooper
Skye Eldora T Bonaby
Alisha Atiya Rolle
Amoss Luafaya Ferguson
Bradesha Talitha Charlton
Ashanti Elizabeth Stuart
Cardrinique Ashley Taylor

182

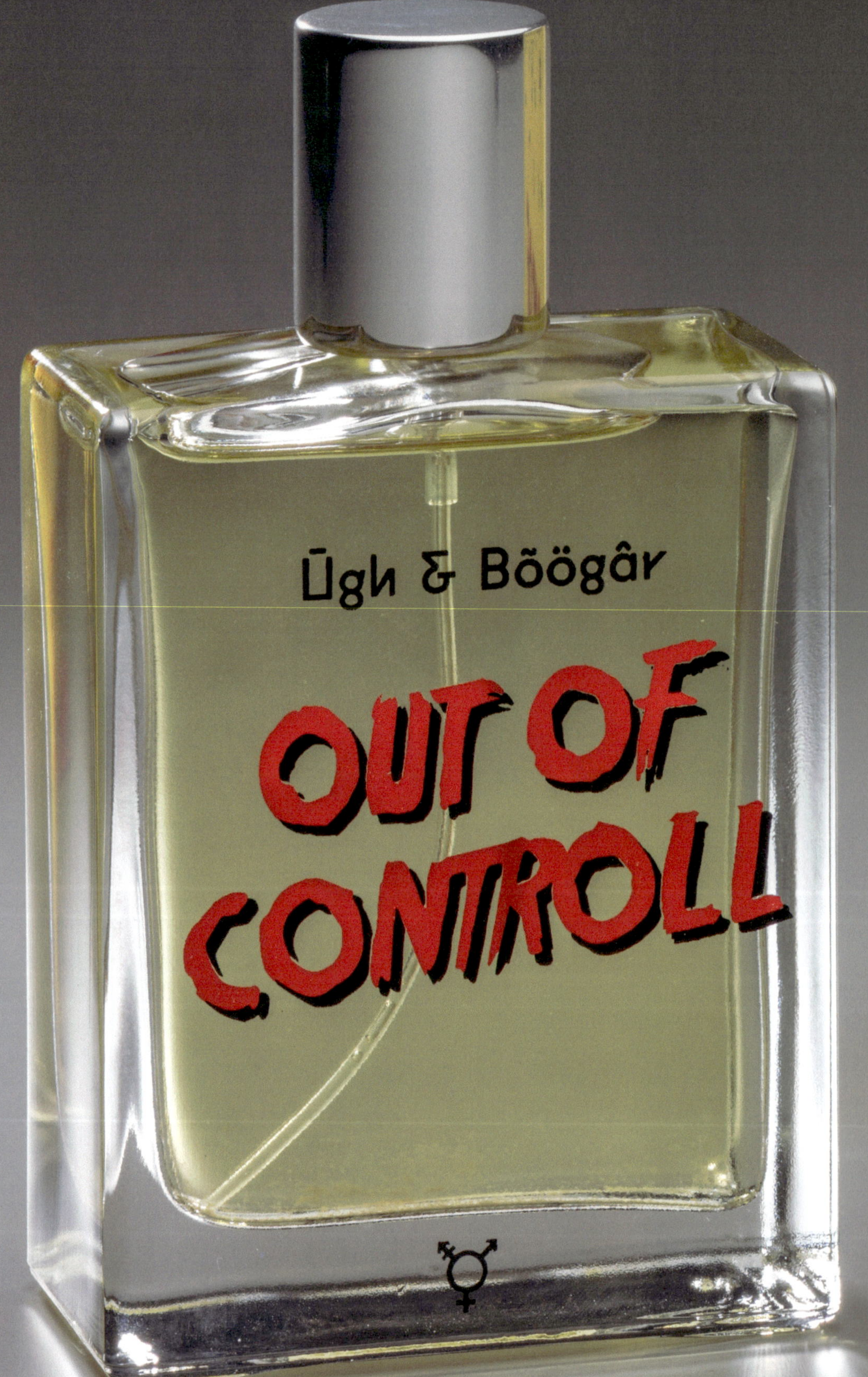

Ūgh & Bõögâr
OUT OF
CONTROLL

Checklist and List of Illustrations

Angolan Pavilion, 2013

Angolan photographer Edson Chagas created *Luanda, Encyclopedic City* for the Angolan Pavilion at the 2013 Biennale. The pavilion, which was the first for a sub-Saharan African country, won the Golden Lion for best national participation. Chagas's photographic series *Found Not Taken* catalogues abandoned objects in Luanda, creating an ambiguous taxonomy of forms and symbols. The installation in Venice included twenty-three stacks of posters, each bearing a different image, that visitors could take away.

> **CAT 1** Posters from *Luanda, Encyclopedic City*
> Edson Chagas (b. Luanda, 1977)
> Each 19 × 27 in. (48.3 × 68.6 cm)
> VB13 NE2698 C433 V45 2013po
> (fig. 4, pp. 14, 28–29 gatefold)

Australian Pavilion, 2015

In 2015, Australian artist Fiona Hall inaugurated her country's new pavilion with *Wrong Way Time*. Her presentation of more than eight hundred objects such as clocks, fantastical camouflaged figures, and international currency in glassy curiosity cabinets was a sober meditation on global politics, finance, and, above all, environmental degradation.

> **CAT 2** Exhibition cards from *Wrong Way Time*
> Fiona Hall (b. Sydney, 1953)
> Each 8 ¼ × 5 ¾ in. (21 × 14.6 cm)
> VB15 NE2698 H175 V45 2015
> (p. 2)

CAT 3 Necklace and pendant from
Wrong Way Time
Fiona Hall (b. Sydney, 1953)
Pendant: 2¾ × 2¼ in. (7 × 5.7 cm);
chain: 17 in. (43.2 cm)
VB15 NE2698 H175 V45 2015n
(fig. 14, p. 45)

CAT 4 Sardine can USB drive from
Wrong Way Time
Fiona Hall (b. Sydney, 1953)
2¼ × 1¼ in. (5.7 × 3.2 cm)
VB15 NE2698 H175 V45 2015p

CAT 5 Tote bag from *Wrong Way Time*
Fiona Hall (b. Sydney, 1953)
18 × 14¾ in. (45.7 × 37.5 cm)
VB15 NE2698 H175 V45 2015b

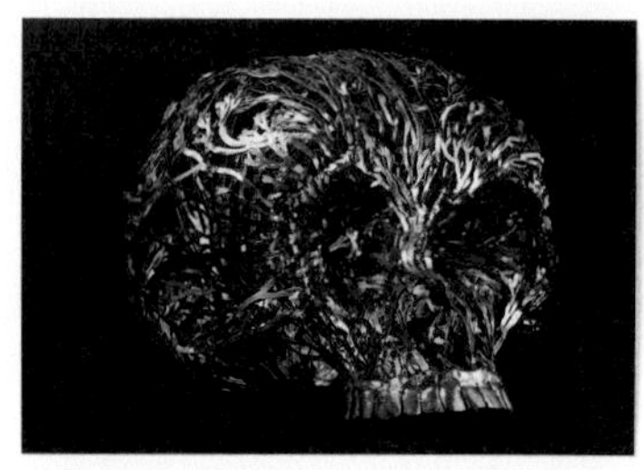

CAT 2

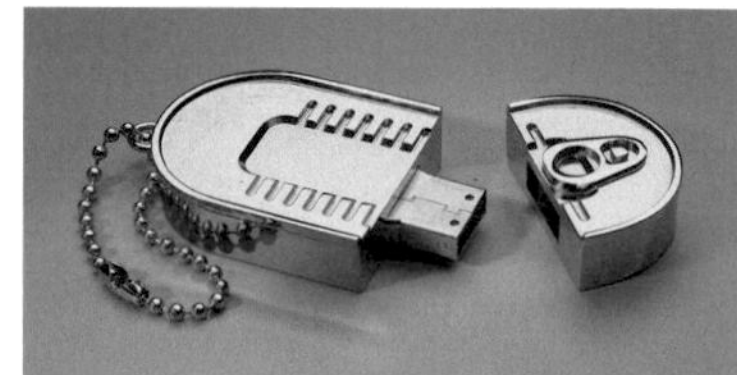

CAT 4

Bahamian Pavilion, 2013

Tavares Strachan, a New York City–based Bahamian artist, has often explored orthostatic tolerance—the body's ability to withstand pressure during the gravitational stress of quick changes in altitude, whether being launched into space or submerged in an ocean's depths. For the first Bahamian Pavilion in Venice, Strachen linked the Arsenale, the North Pole, and Nassau, Bahamas, through an immersive installation documenting a reenactment of a 1909 polar expedition.

CAT 6 Tote bag from *Polar Eclipse*
Tavares Strachan (b. Nassau, 1979)
13⅝ × 12¾ in. (34.6 × 32.4 cm)
VB13 NF302 S894 V45 2013b
(p. 60)

CAT 7 Vinyl record: *40 Days & 40 Nights*
Tavares Strachan (b. Nassau, 1979)
Each 7 × 7 in. (17.8 × 17.8 cm)
VB13 NF302 S894 V45 2013p
(p. 82)

British Pavilion, 2007

Tracey Emin's installation for the British Pavilion encompassed a range of media, from embroidery to drawing and broken-wood sculptures to neon light. As with much of her work, *Borrowed Light* used language and images of intimacy to convey life's emotional complexities.

CAT 8 Booklet and envelope from *Borrowed Light*
Tracey Emin (b. London, 1963)
Booklet: 4⅜ × 3⅛ in. (11 × 8 cm); envelope: 4¾ × 3½ in. (12 × 9 cm)
VB07 ND497 E5 V46 2007e

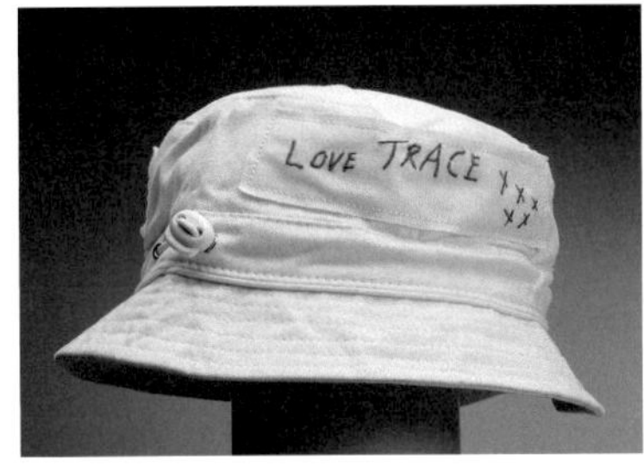

CAT 9

CAT 9 Hat from *Borrowed Light*
Tracey Emin (b. London, 1963)
10 ¼ × 10 ¼ × 4 ¾ in. (26 × 26 × 12 cm)
VB07 ND497 E5 V46 2007h

CAT 10 Temporary tattoo from *Borrowed Light*
Tracey Emin (b. London, 1963)
4 ⅜ × 3 ⅛ in. (11 × 8 cm)
VB07 ND497 E5 V46 2007e

British Pavilion, 2009

For the British Pavilion at the 2009 Biennale, artist Steve McQueen created *Giardini*, a quiet, thirty-minute meditation on the gardens. The two-channel film was shot in February, when the parkland is largely abandoned, and the national pavilions are boarded up. Characterized by mists, sunsets, the sounds of church bells, and other moody material, it is a composition made up of resonant details.

CAT 11 Exhibition catalogue: *Giardini Notebook*
Steve McQueen (b. London, 1969)
6 ½ × 9 ½ in. (16.5 × 9.5 cm)
VB09 NF497 M163 V46 2009
(pp. 78–79 gatefold)

CAT 12 Brochure: *Giardini*
Steve McQueen (b. London, 1969)
8 ½ × 4 ½ in. (21 × 12 cm)
VB09 NF497 M163 V46 2009

British Pavilion, 2013

Jeremy Deller created a multimedia installation titled *English Magic* for the British Pavilion at the 2013 Biennale. As with much of his work, it drew on the country's myths, folklore, and communities, reaching both high and low to explore "magical" transformations in British society. In Deller's time-hopping story, William Morris returns from the dead; a bird of prey seeks revenge on a Range Rover; and a town in the Channel Islands burns.

CAT 13 Artist's book from *English Magic*
Jeremy Deller (b. London, 1966)
8 ½ × 5 ¼ in. (21.6 × 13.3 cm)
AB VB13 NF497 D357 V45 2013e/b
(p. 25)

CAT 14 Prints from *English Magic*
Jeremy Deller (b. London, 1966)
Each 8 ¼ × 11 ⅝ in. (21 × 29.5 cm)
VB13 D357 V45 2013e
(p. 24)

CAT 15 Tote bag from *English Magic*
Jeremy Deller (b. London, 1966)
17 × 14 ½ in. (43.2 × 36.8 cm)
VB13 D357 V45 2013b

Canadian Pavilion, 2011

For his exhibition in Venice, Canadian artist Steven Shearer used figurative painting, drawing, and a large text-based mural on the pavilion's facade to explore the subculture of heavy metal music. The intimacy of his canvases and works on paper contrasts the "antagonistic and bombastic tone" of the poem exhibited outside the pavilion, which was "meant to act as a social leveler" calling "for the destruction of all things equally."

> **CAT 16** Artist-designed magazine: *Conservative Shithead* issue 3
> Steven Shearer (b. New Westminster, 1968)
> 11 ¾ × 8 ¼ in. (29.8 × 21 cm)
> VB11 ND249 S443 V46 2011
> (pp. 30–31)

Collateral Events, 2011

Before the Venice Biennale opens to the public, thousands of artists, art dealers, curators, critics, and other art workers descend upon the city for a week of previews and parties. This invitation is for a party thrown by Larry Gagosian, owner of a worldwide network of galleries, to celebrate the Austrian artist Franz West (1947–2012). In a humorous gesture befitting West's wry artwork, the invitation unfolds to reveal a touristic view of Venice's Grand Canal. Its speaker emits music typically heard on gondolas.

> **CAT 17** Dinner invitation from Gagosian Gallery
> 9 ⅝ × 7 ⅝ in. (24.4 × 19.4 cm)
> VB11 N5146 A7 2011pa
> (fig. 10, p. 41 gatefold)

> **CAT 18** Dinner invitation from Hauser & Wirth
> 4 × 6 in. (10.2 × 15.2 cm)
> VB11 N5146 A7 2011pa

Collateral Project, 2009

In 2009, Palestine's first official contribution to the Biennale was an authorized off-site exhibition entitled *Palestine c/o Venice*. For that exhibition, artist Emily Jacir proposed printing the names of vaporetto (water bus) stops along one route through Venice in both Arabic and Italian. The artwork was Jacir's attempt to put the city's public transportation system in dialogue with the shared European-Arab heritage of its surroundings. It was approved by all relevant authorities, but three months before the Biennale opened, the project was shut down abruptly and without explanation. Nevertheless, Jacir then created the map and brochure presented here—a guide to an artwork that never existed.

> **CAT 19** Exhibition catalogue from *Palestine c/o Venice*
> 11 ⅛ × 9 in. (28.3 × 22.9 cm)
> VB09 N7277 V46 2009

> **CAT 20** Map: *Stazione*
> Emily Jacir (b. Bethlehem, 1970)
> 20 ⅛ × 22 ⅞ in. (51 × 58 cm)
> VB09 NF979 J12 V46 2009
> (fig. 11, p. 42 gatefold)

Collateral Project, 2017

Artist Antoni Abad proposed, with his project for the Catalonian Pavilion at the Venice Biennale, to represent alternative ways of navigating urban environments, whether physical or digital. His *Unveiling the Unseen* took the form of an exhibition, boat tours, and an app that shared the experiences of visually impaired or blind people. It offered a sensorial version of the Italian city, with location-based sound maps and other tools to improve the services to visually impaired citizens and visitors.

> **CAT 21** Artist's book: *Unveiling the Unseen*
> Antoni Abad (Spanish; b. Lleida, 1956)
> 11¾ × 9¼ in. (29.8 × 23.5 cm)
> VB17 NF813 A23 V46 2017

Dutch Pavilion, 2011

The Dutch Pavilion was converted into a kind of theater for the 2011 Venice Biennale. Curator Guus Beumer brought together nearly a dozen artists to examine whether national identity can be reinterpreted through the notion of community, and whether community can be fostered through cultural infrastructure.

> **CAT 22** Pop-up maquette from *Loose Work*
> Maureen Mooren (b. Dordrecht, 1969)
> 9½ × 13 in. (24.1 × 33 cm)
> VB11 N6948 V46 2011
> (p. 8)

> **CAT 23** Printed sheets and booklet from *Loose Work*
> Various artists
> Each 13 × 9½ in. (33 × 24.1 cm)
> VB11 N6948 V46 2011

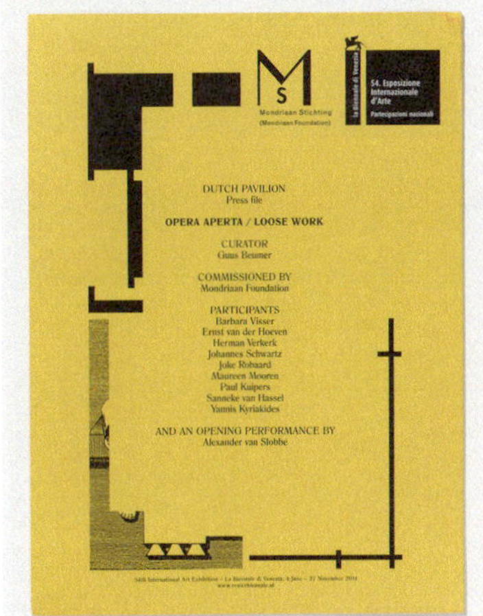

CAT 23

Dutch Pavilion, 2013

Room with Broken Sentence surveyed more than twenty years of Dutch artist Mark Manders's output and included a new monumental sculpture. Its installations, prints, and architectural interventions were enigmatic—materials were not what they seemed—yet visually seductive. The elegant catalogue functions similarly, with personal reflections by nearly forty international writers.

> **CAT 24** Exhibition catalogue: *Mark Manders: Room with Broken Sentence*
> Mark Manders (b. Volkel, 1968)
> 10⅝ × 8¼ in. (27 × 21 cm)
> VB13 NF653 M272 V45 2013

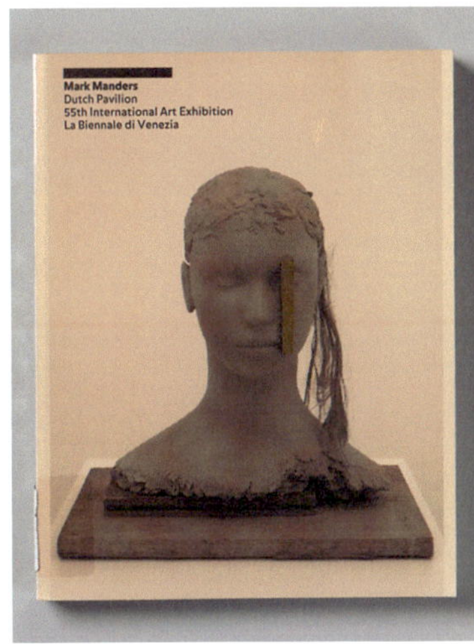

CAT 24

Estonian Pavilion, 2015

Since 2007, Estonian artist Jaanus Samma has collected and exhibited the hidden histories of gay lives in Soviet Estonia. *Not Suitable for Work,* his installation for the Estonian Pavilion at the 2015 Biennale, used the form of a fictional opera to follow the travails of a collective-farm chairman on trial in the 1960s for "acts of homosexuality."

> **CAT 25** Artist's book: *Criminal Case No. 6*, from *Not Suitable for Work: A Chairman's Tale*
> Jaanus Samma (b. Tallinn, 1982)
> 12 ⅜ × 9 ¼ in. (31.4 × 23.5 cm)
> VB15 NF955 E8 S35 V45 2015c
> (pp. 22–23)

> **CAT 26** Tote bag from *Not Suitable for Work: A Chairman's Tale*
> Jaanus Samma (b. Tallinn, 1982)
> 16 ¼ × 14 ¾ in. (41.3 37.5 cm)
> VB15 NF955 E8 S35 V45 2015b

> **CAT 27** Brochure: *Not Suitable for Work: A Chairman's Tale*
> Jaanus Samma (b. Tallinn, 1982)
> 5 ⅞ × 4 ⅜ in. (15 × 11 cm)
> VB15 NF955 E8 S35 V45 2017e

Finnish Pavilion, 2017

This is the elegant and laboriously designed artist book that accompanied Nathaniel Mellors and Erkka Nissinen's installation in the Finnish Pavilion at the 2017 Biennale. Their exhibition involved video, animatronics, and the participation of Finnish celebrities to offer an absurd but pointed examination of Finnish identity. The book's cover mimics a scene in the video in which a guitar-playing figure has a box with eyeholes for a head.

> **CAT 28** Exhibition catalogue: *The Aalto Natives: A Transcendental Manual*
> Nathaniel Mellors (British; b. Doncaster, 1974) and Erkka Nissinen
> (b. Jyväskylä, 1975)
> 11 ¾ × 8 ⅝ in. (29.9 × 21.9 cm)
> VB17 NF955 F53 N57 V46 2017
> (pp. 54–57, gatefolds)

French Pavilion, 2011

For decades, artist Christian Boltanski has explored fate through installations that use light and accumulations of objects to meditate on disappearance and death. For the French Pavilion at the 2011 Biennale, Boltanski turned to another form of chance: birth. A large, mechanical installation filled the Neoclassical pavilion with a whirring "filmstrip" printed with newborns' faces. This contraption would pause occasionally, and a baby's face would be spot lit on monitors.

> **CAT 29** Posters from *Chance*
> Christian Boltanski (b. Paris, 1944)
> Each 16 ½ × 24 in. (41.9 × 61 cm)
> VB11 NE2698 B694 V46 2011p
> (fig. 13, p. 44)

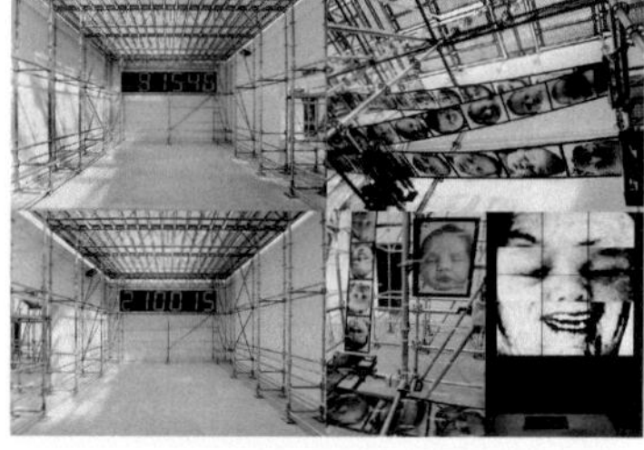

CAT 29

  CHECKLIST AND LIST OF ILLUSTRATIONS

Greek Pavilion, 2015

Artist Maria Papadimitriou built a to-scale replica of a shop selling animal hides and leather for her presentation at the 2015 Venice Biennale. *Why Look at Animals? AGRIMIKÁ* underscored humans' anthropocentric worldview by meditating upon the kinds of animals, such as wolves, that coexist with people but cannot be domesticated by them. This relationship was presented as an allegory of the dispossessed and the resistant at a moment when Greek society was roiled by economic challenges and issues pertaining to immigration and migration.

> **CAT 30** Cowbell from *Why Look at Animals? AGRIMIKÁ*
> Maria Papadimitriou (b. Athens, 1957)
> 3 × 2 ⅝ in. (7.6 × 6.7 cm)
> VB15 NF603 P213 V46 2015c
> (p. 34)

Icelandic Pavilion, 2015

In 2015, Iceland's pavilion was located in the Santa Maria della Misericordia, a former Catholic church that had been unused for decades. Swiss artist Christoph Büchel proposed turning the building into the first functioning mosque in central Venice for the duration of the Biennale. The project was intended to highlight the influence of Islamic trade and culture on the city. The installation lasted only two weeks before it was shut down by the police, whose letters declaring it closed are included in the exhibition.

> **CAT 31** Police notices, flyer, and donation form from *THE MOSQUE: The First Mosque in the Historic City of Venice*
> Christoph Büchel (Swiss; b. Basel, 1966)
> Police notices: each 11 ⅝ × 8 ¼ in. (29.5 × 21 cm); flyer: 8 ¼ × 5 ¾ in. (21 × 14.6 cm); donation form: 5 ⅞ × 8 ¼ in (14.9 × 21 cm)
> VB15 NF853 B919 V46 2015p
> (fig. 15, p. 46)

Icelandic Pavilion, 2017

For the Icelandic Pavilion at the 2017 Biennale, artist Egill Sæbjörnsson invented Ūgh and Bõõgâr, two trolls whose interests determined the pavilion's varied contents. Sæbjörnsson and his trolls collaborated on music; worked with perfumer Gez Schön on a custom scent; created clothes with an award-winning Icelandic fashion designer; and created large-scale video installations and functional clay sculptures.

> **CAT 32** Café materials from *Out of Controll in Venice*
> Egill Sæbjörnsson (b. Reykjavik, 1973)
> Napkin: 4 ¾ × 4 ½ in. (12.1 × 11.4 cm); sugar packets: each 1 ¾ × 2 ¾ in. (4.4 × 7 cm)
> VB17 ND753 E35.3 V46 2017c

> **CAT 33** Perfume bottle from *Out of Controll in Venice*
> Egill Sæbjörnsson (b. Reykjavik, 1973)
> 4 ½ × 2 ⅝ × 1 ½ in. (4.4 × 6.7 × 3.8 cm)
> VB17 ND753 E35.3 V46 2017e
> (p. 84)

CAT 34 Pins from *Out of Controll in Venice*
Egill Sæbjörnsson (b. Reykjavik, 1973)
Each diameter: 1 in. (2.5 cm)
VB17 ND753 E35.3 V46 2017p

CAT 35 Vinyl record from *Out of Controll in Venice*
Egill Sæbjörnsson (b. Reykjavik, 1973)
12 ⅜ × 12 ⅜ in. (31.4 × 31.4 cm)
VB17 ND753 E35.3 V46 2017r

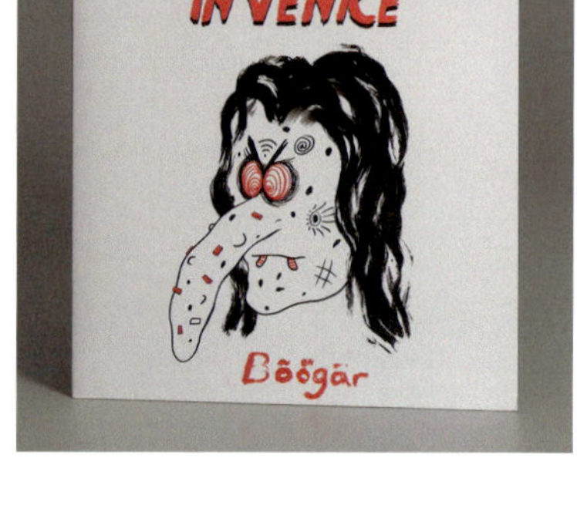

CAT 35

Korean Pavilion, 2017

For the 2017 Biennale, curator Lee Daehyung brought together works by artists Cody Choi and Lee Wan under the title *Counterbalance: The Stone and the Mountain*. The exhibition was an exercise in understanding how individual stories relate to national histories. Choi often responds to the influence of Western culture through appropriation and parody. Wan investigates economic and social systems through performance and archival research. "By revealing the transnational conditions of production and consumption," Daehyung wrote, "these two artists create . . . distillations of human experience. [. . .] Single stories retain the power to critique and dislodge dominant systems."

CAT 36 Artist's book: *Mr. K*
Lee Wan (b. Seoul, 1979)
11 ¾ × 8 ½ in. (30 × 21.6 cm)
VB17 N7365 V46 2017w
(p. 52)

CAT 37 Artist's book: *Venetian Rhapsody: The Power of Bluff*
Cody Choi (b. Seoul, 1961)
10 ⅝ × 8 ⅛ in. (27 × 20.6 cm)
VB17 N7365 V46 2017c
(p. 53)

CAT 38 Artist's newspaper: *The Counterbalance*
Cody Choi (b. Seoul, 1961)
17 ⅜ × 11 ⅜ in. (44.1 × 28.9 cm)
VB17 N7365 V46 2017ne

CAT 39 Artist's newspaper: *The Counterbalance*
Lee Wan (b. Seoul, 1979)
17 ⅜ × 11 ⅜ in. (44.1 × 28.9 cm)
VB17 N7365 V46 2017ne

CAT 40 Exhibition catalogue: *Counterbalance: The Stone and the Mountain*
Cody Choi (b. Seoul, 1961) and Lee Wan (b. Seoul, 1979)
9 ½ × 6 ⅝ in. (24.1 × 16.8 cm)
VB17 N7365 V46 2017

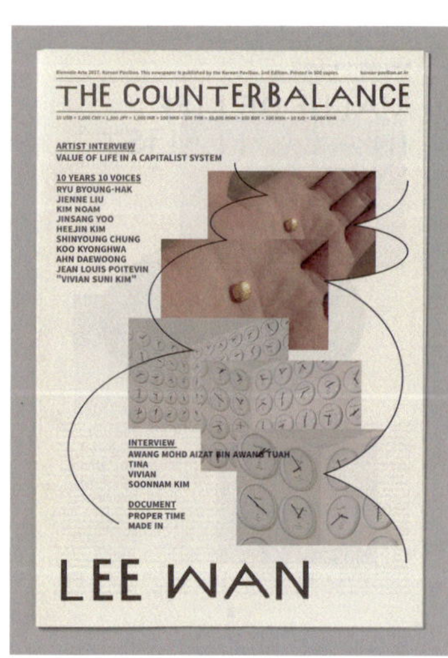

CAT 39

CAT 41 Poker chip USB drive from *Counterbalance: The Stone and the Mountain*
Diameter: 1⅜ in. (3.5 cm)
VB17 N7365 V46 2017p

Lebanese Pavilion, 2013

Akram Zaatari's installation at the 2013 Venice Biennale included a forty-five-minute video, a 16-mm film, and an immersive environment conceived as a stage awaiting an actor. The works centered on the story of an Israeli pilot who in 1982 refused to drop a bomb on a school building in Sayda, the artist's hometown. The story circulated through Lebanon as a rumor for decades; only in 2010 was the story confirmed. Zaatari's art often involves exploring photographic archives and practices as a way of understanding social codes; this newsprint publication is one manifestation of Zaatari's project, which reflects on the complexities of refusal as a generative act.

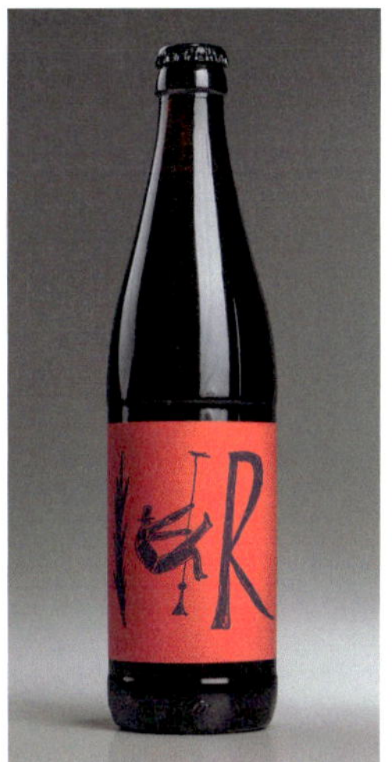

CAT 43

CAT 42 Artist publication from *Letter to a Refusing Pilot*
Akram Zaatari (b. Sayda, 1966)
16⅞ × 11 in. (42.9 × 27.9 cm)
VB13 NE2698 Z38 V45 2013
(pp. 32–33)

Lithuanian Pavilion, 2017

Žilvinas Landzbergas's exhibition, titled *R*, revealed how fantastical and mesmeric aspects of the landscape are an important component of Baltic and Nordic society. His multimedia presentation, which included large-scale sculptures, installations, artist-designed clothing, and other media included "devoured suns and fake moons . . . [sprouting] furniture and giant heads," music, food, and acupuncture sessions.

CAT 43 Beer bottle from *R*
Žilvinas Landzbergas (b. Kaunas, 1979)
Height: 10⅜ in. (26.4 cm); base diameter:
2½ in. (6.3 cm)
VB17 NB955 L573 Z55 V46 2017b

Main Exhibition, 2007

Christine Hill, an American artist who has divided her time between New York and Berlin since 1992, is known for creating the *Volksboutique* workshop, a second-hand shop and social sculpture that has inhabited both urban storefronts and prestigious international exhibitions. For artistic director Robert Storr's main exhibition at the 2007 Venice Biennale, Hill created an installation documented by this book, which intersperses writing by well-known authors with re-creations of her Moleskine documenting the year she had to create her work for Venice.

CAT 44 Artist's book: *Minutes*
Christine Hill (American; b. Binghamton, 1968)
8⅜ × 5⅜ in. (21.3 × 13.7 cm)
VB07 NF237 H645 V46 2007
(fig. 1, p. 10)

Main Exhibition, 2017

Taiwanese-American artist Lee Mingwei's performance as part of the main exhibition of the 2017 Biennale was sited in a small garden inside the central pavilion. It included an empty chair with a stone on its seat. When a visitor entered, a woman in a white robe appeared, removed the stone, and invited the guest to sit. After brief remarks, she left and returned with a letter on a tray like the one seen here. The recipient is instructed to open the envelope "whenever beauty visits."

> **CAT 45** Envelope and letter from *When Beauty Visits*
> Lee Mingwei (b. 1964)
> Envelope: 8 × 6 in. (20.3 × 15.2 cm); letter: 5 ¾ × 7 ¾ in. (14.6 × 19.7 cm)
> VB17 NF237 L479 V46 2017
> (pp. 74–75)

Maldives Pavilion, 2013

Portable Nation, an exhibition curated by Chamber of Public Secrets (Alfredo Cramerotti, Aida Eltorie, and Khaled Ramadan), was the first official presentation by The Maldives at the Venice Biennale. The Ministry of Tourism, Arts, and Culture, which commissioned the pavilion, viewed the Biennale as an opportunity to bring attention to the nation's imperiled status. Rising sea levels caused by climate change threaten to submerge the island; as such, the pavilion was conceived as an "eco-aesthetic space" and a platform for not only artists, but also environmental activists and theorists.

> **CAT 46** Poster from *Portable Nation: Disappearance as Work in Progress, Approaches to Ecological Romanticism*
> 33 × 12 in. (83.8 × 30.5 cm)
> VB13 N7310.8 M415 V46 2013e

> **CAT 47** Printed paper: *The Ice Monolith*
> Stefano Cagol (Italian; b. Trento, 1969)
> 8 ¼ × 11 ¾ in. (21 × 30 cm)
> VB13 N7310.8 M415 V46 2013e

> **CAT 48** Printed paper: *For a Completely Different Climate*
> Oliver Ressler (Austrian; b. Knittelfeld, 1970)
> 8 ¼ × 11 ¾ in. (21 × 30 cm)
> VB13 N7310.8 M415 V46 2013e

> **CAT 49** Printed paper: *Maldives: To Be or Not*
> Khaled Ramadan (Lebanese; b. Beirut, 1965)
> 8 ¼ × 11 ¾ in. (21 × 30 cm)
> VB13 N7310.8 M415 V46 2013e

> **CAT 50** Printed paper: *Pantheistic Polifacetic*
> Patrizio Travagli (Italian; b. Florence, 1972)
> 8 ¼ × 11 ¾ in. (21 × 30 cm)
> VB13 N7310.8 M415 V46 2013e

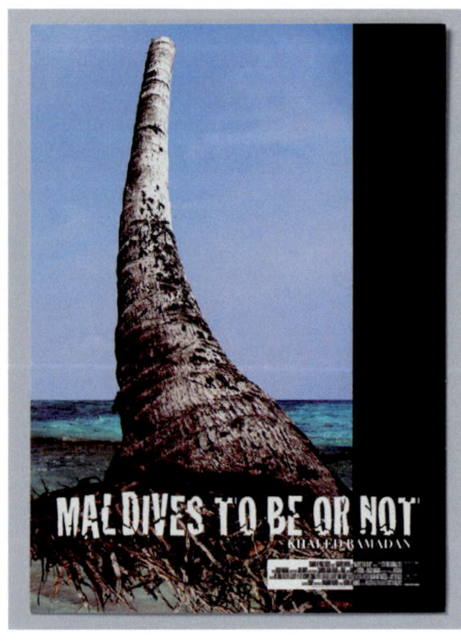

CAT 49

CHECKLIST AND LIST OF ILLUSTRATIONS

CAT 51 Printed paper: *Polar Tide: Floods of Data, Floods of Tones*
Greg Niemeyer (Swiss; b. 1967), Chris Chafe (Swiss; b. Bern, 1952), Perrin Meyer
(American; b. Berkeley)
8 ¼ × 11 ¾ in. (21 × 30 cm)
VB13 N7310.8 M415 V46 2013e

Nordic Pavilion, 2009
For the 2009 Biennale, the Nordic Committee and the Danish Arts Council
commissioned artists Michael Elmgreen and Ingar Dragset to organize the Danish
and Nordic Pavilions. Rather than present an exhibition of only their own work,
Elmgreen and Dragset created *The Collectors*, two fictional worlds centered on
the adjacent buildings, and invited other artists to help them populate it.
Elmgreen and Dragset conceived of each pavilion as a home—the Danish Pavilion
as the setting for a family, the Nordic Pavilion as a bachelor pad. The Danish
Pavilion was "for sale," and a performer acting as a real-estate agent led groups
through the building while relating stories about the inhabitants. In the Nordic
Pavilion, young men sipped drinks and lounged in the fashionable environment.
The pavilion involved more than twenty artists and designers, many of whom
contributed small-scale editioned artworks included in the exhibition.

CAT 52 Artist's book: *Things and Things: From Trains to Paintings*
Dorothea von Hantelmann (German; b. Hamburg, 1969)
5 ⅞ × 4 ½ in. (14.9 × 11.4 cm)
VB09 N7018 V46 2009

CAT 53 Artist's book with paper dolls: *Between Object and Organ:
Powerless Collections*
Clémentine Deliss (British; b. London, 1960)
Book: 6 ¼ × 4 ¾ in. (15.9 × 12.1 cm); dolls: 15 × 10 ⅝ in. (38.1 × 27 cm)
VB09 N7018 V46 2009
(p. 5)

CAT 54 Brochure: *Vigilante Exclusive Real Estate*
Michael Elmgreen (Danish; b. Copenhagen, 1961) and Ingar Dragset
(Norwegian; b. Trondheim, 1969)
9 ¾ × 7 in. (24.8 × 17.8 cm)
VB09 N7018 V46 2009br
(pp. 26–27 gatefold)

CAT 55 Business card: *Vigilante Exclusive Real Estate*
Michael Elmgreen (Danish; b. Copenhagen, 1961) and Ingar Dragset
(Norwegian; b. Trondheim, 1969)
2 ⅛ × 3 ½ in. (5.4 × 8.9 cm)
VB09 N7018 V46 2009bu
(p. 27 gatefold)

CAT 56 Dinner plates: *Table for Bergman*
Michael Elmgreen (Danish; b. Copenhagen, 1961) and Ingar Dragset
(Norwegian; b. Trondheim, 1969)
Each diameter: 12 in. (30.5 cm)
Collection of the artists

CAT 66 Napkin: *Forty Winks*
Vibeke Slyngstad (Norwegian; b. Ålesund, 1968)
8 ¾ × 8 ¾ in. (30 × 30 cm)
VB09 N7018 V46 2009fo

CAT 67 Placemat: *Scribbles, Dribbles, Nibbles*, from *The Collectors*
Simon Fujiwara (British; b. London, 1982)
11½ × 16¼ in. (29.2 × 41.3 cm)
VB09 N7018 V46 2009sc

CAT 68 Postcards from *The Collectors*
Martin Jacobson (Swedish; b. Stockholm, 1978)
Each 3½ × 5½ in. (8.9 × 14 cm)
VB09 N7018 V46 2009

CAT 69 Letters from the United States Department of Agriculture
Each 8½ × 11 in. (22 × 28 cm)
(fig. 3, p. 12)

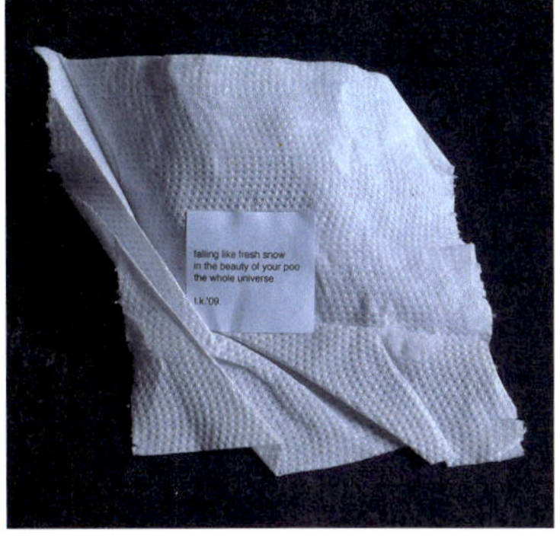
CAT 72

CAT 70 Sign: *Anything Helps*, from *The Collectors*
Jani Leinonen (Finnish; b. Hyvinkää, 1978)
5 × 11 in. (12.7 × 27.9 cm)
VB09 N7018 V46 2009a

CAT 71 Temporary tattoo: *Seller's Aid (I BUY)*, from *The Collectors*
Hernan Bas (American; b. Miami, 1978)
2½ × 3½ in. (6.4 × 8.9 cm)
VB09 N7018 V46 2009s

CAT 72 Toilet Paper: *The Whole Universe*
Terence Koh (Chinese; b. Beijing, 1977)
4⅝ × 4¾ in. (11.7 × 12.1 cm)
VB09 N7018 V46 2009w

Polish Pavilion, 2011
Israeli artist Yael Bartana's installation for the Polish Pavilion at the 2011 Biennale included several films, shot in Warsaw, that imagined a Jewish Renaissance Movement. Its manifesto includes the statement: "We will accept anyone into our ranks for whom there was no room in their homelands—the expelled, persecuted. [. . .] We will be strong in our weakness."

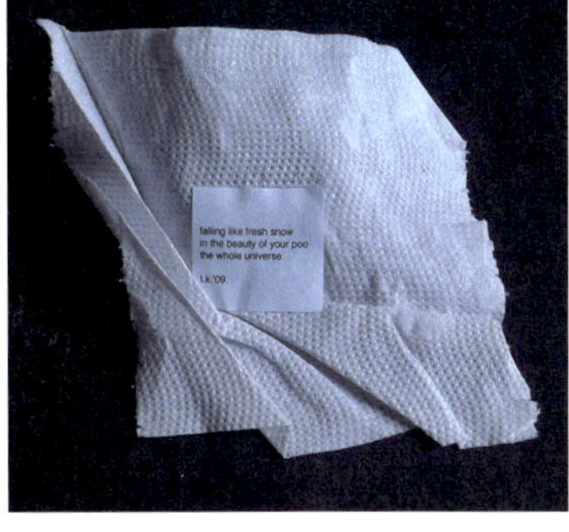
CAT 73

CAT 73 Exhibition catalogue: *A Cook Book for Political Imagination*, from *. . . And Europe will be Stunned*
Yael Bartana (Israeli; b. Kfar Yehezkel, 1970)
8½ × 5¾ × 1⅞ in. (21.6 × 14.6 × 4.8 cm)
VB11 N7255 P6 V46 2011

CAT 74 Membership card for *The Jewish Renaissance Movement*, from *. . . And Europe will be Stunned*
Yael Bartana (Israeli; b. Kfar Yehezkel, 1970)
2 ³⁄₁₆ × 3 ⁵⁄₁₆ in. (5.6 × 8.4 cm)
VB11 N7255 P6 V46 2011c

CAT 75 Invitation for *The Jewish Renaissance Movement in Poland*, from *. . . And Europe will be Stunned*
Yael Bartana (Israeli; b. Kfar Yehezkel, 1970)
8 × 5 ¾ in. (20.3 × 14.6 cm)
VB11 N7255 P6 V46 2011p

CAT 76 Poster for *The Jewish Renaissance Movement in Poland*, from *. . . And Europe will be Stunned*
Yael Bartana (Isareli; b. Kfar Yehezkel, 1970)
8 ¼ × 5 ⅞ in. (21 × 15 cm)
VB11 N7255 P6 V46 2011p
(pp. 58–59)

Polish Pavilion, 2013

The focal point of Konrad Smoleński's installation in the Polish Pavilion was a sculptural instrument composed of two large bells, a stack of loudspeakers, and other resonating objects. The artist composed a delay-heavy composition for these instruments that contrasts the tolling of the bells with abstract noise.

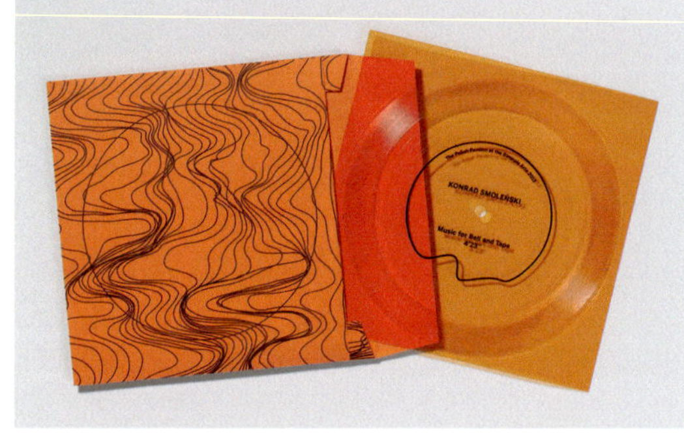

CAT 77

CAT 77 Flexidisc: *Music for Bell and Tape*
Konrad Smoleński (b. Kalisz, 1977)
7 × 7 in. (17.8 × 17.8 cm)
VB13 NF955 P63 S666 V46 2013p

CAT 78 Brochure: *Everything Was Forever, Until It Was No More*
Konrad Smolenski (b. Kalisz, 1977)
6 ¾ × 5 ½ in. (17 × 14 cm)
VB13 NF955 P63 S666 V46 2013p

Slovenian Pavilion, 2013

For Our Economy and Culture, Jasmina Cibic's installation in the Slovenian Pavilion at the 2013 Venice Biennale, included videos, a performance, photographs, and this wallpaper. The Slovenian beetle depicted here was discovered by explorer Vladimir Kodrič in 1933; four years later, entomologist Oskar Scheibel confirmed the discovery of the new species and, as a Nazi supporter, named it *Anophthalmus hitleri*. The varied depictions were created by forty international scientific illustrators who, at Cibic's request, drew the beetle with no reference beyond its name and their own experiences in the field. Because of its name, which prompts collectors of Hitler memorabilia to seek it out, the beetle is now on the endangered species list.

CAT 79 Printed wallpaper: *The Fruits of Our Land*
Jasmina Cibic (b. Ljubljana, 1979)
20 ½ in. × 33 ft. (52.1 cm × 10 m)
VB13 NE2698 C567 V45 2013w
(p. 83)

Swiss Pavilion, 2011

The group exhibition *Chewing the Scenery* used time-based art and writing to explore "delays, leaps and ruptures, anachronisms and dissonance" in contemporary society. The presentation included a film installation, a dramatization featuring four actors in the same role, and live events. The publication engages the theme in its structure: not only are its pages loose, but it was also expanded, reworked, and reissued twice during the exhibition.

CAT 80 Exhibition publication: *Chewing the Scenery*
Maria Iorio (b. Lausanne, 1975), Raphaël Cuomo (b. Delemont, 1977), Uriel Orlow (b. Zurich, 1973), and Eran Schaerf (Israeli; b. Tel Aviv, 1962)
15 × 10 ¼ in. (38.1 × 26 cm)
VB11 N7148 V46 2011
(pp. 76–77)

Swiss Pavilion, 2013

Visitors to Valentin Carron's Swiss Pavilion in 2013 were greeted by the forked tongue of a snake; its body, rendered in steel, extended more than two hundred and fifty feet and wound through the installation. A series of fiberglass works inspired by stained glass in mid-century public and religious architecture recall abstract paintings. Several sculptures of flattened instruments and other works rounded out the artist's meditation on sculpture as a medium.

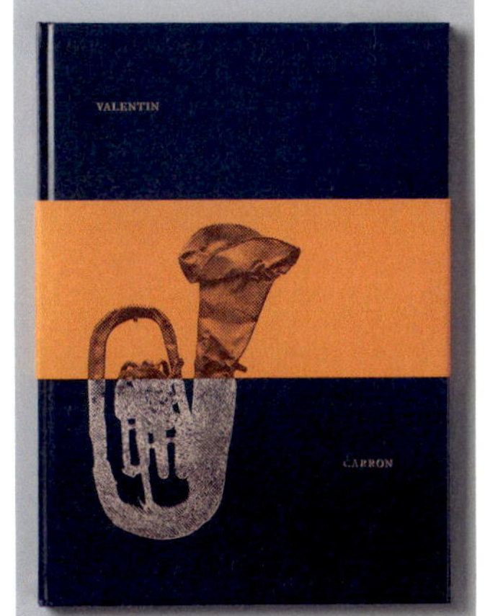
CAT 81

CAT 81 Artist's book: *Valentin Carron*
Valentin Carron (b. Martigny, 1977)
12 ¾ × 9 ¼ in. (32.4 × 23.5 cm)
VB13 NB853 C28 V45 2013

Tunisian Pavilion, 2017

The Absence of Paths, which was installed in kiosks throughout Venice, involved a physical travel document called a Freesa, which was made in collaboration with a company that produces identification papers for countries around the world. This performance piece juxtaposes "the cold mechanics of immigration bureaucracy" with "an imagined world free of borders."

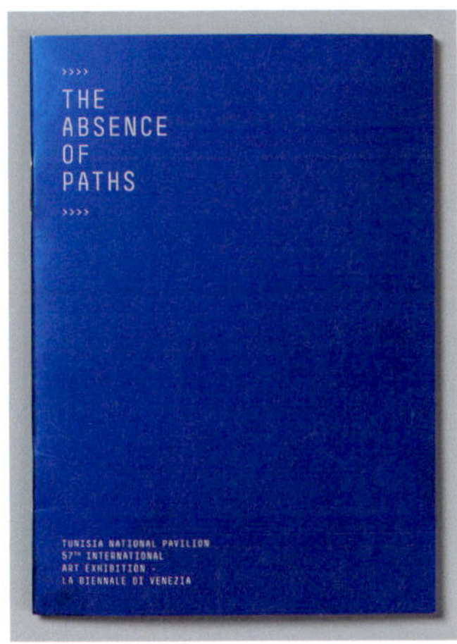

CAT 82

CAT 82 Booklet and Freesa from *The Absence of Paths*
Booklet: 6 ¾ × 4 in. (17.1 × 10.2 cm); freesa: 3 ¼ × 4 ½ in. (8.3 × 11.4 cm)
VB17 N7391 V46 2017f
(fig. 7, p. 19)

CAT 83 Application form from *The Absence of Paths*
5¾ × 3 in. (14.6 × 7.6 cm)
VB17 N7391 V46 2017f
(fig. 7, p. 18)

United Arab Emirates Pavilion, 2015

The exhibition this catalogue accompanies was built on extensive research into the recent history of art in the United Arab Emirates. It presented artworks from several decades that emerged from or were related to the Emirates Fine Arts Society, a nonprofit association established in Sharjah in 1980.

CAT 84 Exhibition catalogue: *1980–Today: Exhibitions in the United Arab Emirates*
10⅛ × 7⅛ in. (25.7 × 18.1 cm)
VB15 N3810 U6 V46 2015nc
(pp. 80–81 gatefold)

Unsanctioned Event, 2017

In 2017, University of the Arts Helsinki, an interdisciplinary arts school in Finland, sponsored the second Research Pavilion as a collateral event of the Venice Biennale. *Utopia of Access* included three exhibitions and more than forty interdisciplinary events that involved more than one hundred artists and researchers from across Europe.

CAT 85 Lenticular postcard for *You Gotta Say Yes to Another Access*, from *Utopia of Access*
Mareia C. Saladrigues (Spanish, b. Terrassa, 1978)
4 × 6 in. (10.2 × 15.2 cm)
VB17 N6493.5 V46 2017re

Unsanctioned Project, 2015

During the opening of the 2015 Venice Biennale, a group of anonymous Ukrainian artists occupied the Russian Pavilion to protest Russia's annexation of Crimea. Wearing camouflage fatigues, these artists urged visiting tourists to put on the uniforms and take selfies in "the occupying power of [their] choice." Posting those images to social media offered a chance to win a vacation to seaside Crimean town of Balaklava.

CAT 86 Jacket from *#ONVACATION*
Anonymous artists
33¼ × 27½ in.; sleeve length: 26¼ in. (84.5 × 69.9 cm; sleeve length: 66.7 cm)
VB15 N7255 U47 O5 V46 2015j
(fig. 6, p. 16)

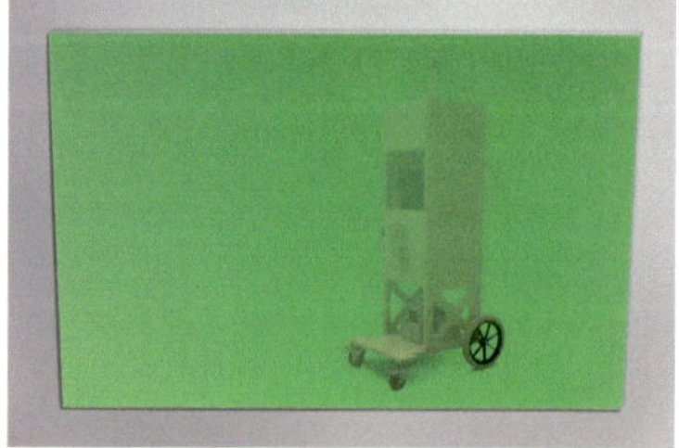
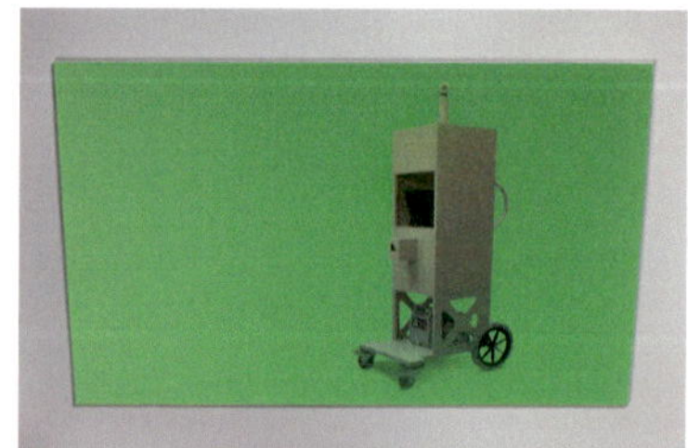

CAT 85

Unsanctioned Projects, 2017
The NSK State Pavilion is one of several recent Biennale projects that render literal questions of identity, migration, borders, and access. It involved offering visitors a Neue Slowenische Kunst (NSK) passport that identified the bearer as a citizen of the NSK state. *The Boat Is Leaking. The Captain Lied*, an exhibition featuring esteemed artists working in different disciplines, was the Fondazione Prada's presentation in Venice during the 2017 Biennale.

Several objects collected during the 58th Venice Biennale (2019) were included in *Art's Biggest Stage*, but these objects had not been selected at the time of publication.

Contributors

Sarah Hamerman is an art librarian and researcher based in New Jersey. She is the poetry cataloguing specialist at Princeton University Rare Books and Special Collections. Previously she was assistant librarian at the Whitney Museum Library and project cataloguer for artists' books at the MoMA Library. Sarah is also a founding member of the Cybernetics Library. She holds an MSLIS/MS in art history from the Pratt Institute, New York (2017). Her writing and curatorial interests include artists' engagements with library and archival systems, experimental publishing, and artists' networks. Sarah's writing has appeared in *Art Libraries Journal*, *Temporary Art Review*, and *Avant.org*, among other publications. She has co-organized exhibitions and programs at the Schinkel Pavilion, the Internet Archive, and the New York Art Book Fair.

Susan Roeper is director of the library at the Sterling and Francine Clark Art Institute. Her research and collection development interests include contemporary art, photography, illustrated books, and artists' books. She has overseen the collecting of materials related to the Venice Biennale since 2007. Among Roeper's most recent projects is the installation of the Allan Sekula Library in the Manton Research Center at the Clark.

Brian Sholis is an independent curator, editor, and writer in Toronto. Prior to working independently, he was executive director of the non-profit Gallery TPW in Toronto; curator of photography at the Cincinnati Art Museum; and an editor at Aperture Foundation and *Artforum*. A specialist in contemporary art and photography, Sholis organized the 2016–17 exhibition *Kentucky Renaissance: The Lexington Camera Club and Its Community, 1954–1974* and authored its accompanying catalogue. He has written catalogue essays for the Museum of Modern Art, the Whitney Museum of American Art, and the New Museum in New York; the Moderna Museet in Stockholm; the Hayward Gallery in London; and the Tel Aviv Museum of Art, among other institutions. A longtime art critic, his essays, columns, interviews, and reviews have appeared in *Artforum*, *Frieze*, *Art in America*, *Aperture*, and other publications.

This book is published on the occasion of the exhibition *Art's Biggest Stage: Collecting the Venice Biennale, 2007–2019* presented at the Clark Art Institute from July 4 to October 14, 2019.

The Clark's summer 2019 exhibitions and programs are made possible in part by generous support from Denise Littlefield Sobel. Support for *Art's Biggest Stage: Collecting the Venice Biennale, 2007–2019* is provided by Maureen Fennessy Bousa and Edward P. Bousa and Amy and Charlie Scharf, with additional support from the Rohit and Katharine Desai Family Foundation.

Published by the Publications Department of the Clark Art Institute
225 South Street
Williamstown, MA 01267
clarkart.edu

Anne Roecklein, Managing Editor
Kevin Bicknell, Editor
Samantha Page, Publications Assistant

Produced by Lucia | Marquand, Seattle
luciamarquand.com

Copyedited by Melissa Duffes
Designed by Ryan Polich
Typeset by Tina Henderson
Proofread by Barbara Bowen
Printed and bound in China by Artron Art Printing

Distributed by Yale University Press
302 Temple Street
P.O. Box 209040
New Haven, CT 06520-9040
yalebooks.com/art

10 9 8 7 6 5 4 3 2 1

Library of Congress Cataloging-in-Publication Data

Names: Sterling and Francine Clark Art Institute, author. | Sholis, Brian. International departures. | Hamerman, Sarah. Archiving the now. | Roeper, Susan, 1957–. Collecting the Biennale.
Title: Art's biggest stage : collecting the Venice Bienniale, 2007–2019 / Brian Sholis ; with contributions by Sarah Hamerman and Susan Roeper.
Description: Williamstown, Massachusetts : Clark Art Institute, 2019. | "This publication was published by the Clark Art Institute on the occasion of the exhibition Art's Biggest Stage: Collecting the Venice Biennale, 2007–2019, Clark Art Institute, Williamstown, Massachusetts, July 4–October 14, 2019." | Includes bibliographical references and index.
Identifiers: LCCN 2019013156 | ISBN 9780300246896 (hardcover) | ISBN 9781935998402 (clark art institute)
Subjects: LCSH: Biennale di Venezia—Library resources. | Sterling and Francine Clark Art Institute. Library. | Art, Modern—21st century—Exhibitions. | Art libraries—Collection development—Massachusetts—Williamstown. | BISAC: ART / History / Contemporary (1945–). | ART / Collections, Catalogs, Exhibitions / Permanent Collections.
Classification: LCC Z5935.5 .S56 2019 N5073.V4 | DDC 025.2/1867—dc23
LC record available at https://lccn.loc.gov/2019013156

Image credits:
Title spread: cat. 2; p. 5: cat. 53; p. 8: cat. 22; p. 34: cat. 30; p. 60: cat. 6; p. 84: cat. 33

Unless otherwise noted, images of objects in the Clark's library collection are by Mike Agee. Additional credits are as follows: Amanda Merullo for the *New York Times*: fig. 2; © Edson Chagas, courtesy of the artist and APALAZZOGALLERY, photo: Paolo Utimperger: fig. 4; Marco Secchi/ Getty Images: fig. 9; © Allora & Calzadilla, courtesy of the Lisson Gallery, photo: Tascha Horowitz, courtesy of the Indianapolis Museum of Art: fig. 12; © 2019 Artists Rights Society (ARS), New York, photo: Moira Ricci: fig. 16; Photo: Archivo Storico della Biennale di Venezia–Asac: fig. 17; © 2019 Joan Jonas/Artists Rights Society (ARS), New York, Photo: Moira Ricci: fig. 19; © Joana Hadjithomas and Khalil Joreige. Photo courtesy the artists and In Situ – fabienne leclerc: fig. 21